The Wonders of Tariqa Kasnazāniyya Brought to India

Compilation, Editing, and Introduction

Dr Louay Fatoohi

THE WAY PUBLISHING

Production Reference: 1180815

First published: August 2015
by The Way Publishing
Birmingham, UK.
www.thewaypublish.com

ISBN 978-1-906342-22-7 (Paperback)
ISBN 978-1-906342-23-4 (E-book)
1. Religion : Islam – Sufi 2. Religion : Islam – General 3. Religion : Mysticism

The cover photo and design are by Mawlid Design www.mawliddesign.com.

In the name of Allah, the Compassionate, the Merciful

Those who say "Allah is our Lord" and then follow the straight path will have angels descend on them [saying]: "Do not fear and do not grieve, but have the good news of paradise, which you have been promised. We are your allies in this world and the hereafter. You will have in it whatever your souls desire and you will have in it whatever you request — a gift sent down from One who is forgiving, merciful" (*Qur'an, 41.30-32*)

O Allah! Send prayer on our Master Muḥammad whose attributes, revelation, message, and wisdom are most praised, and on his lineage and companions, and salute them with a perfect salutation. (*Al-Waṣfiyya Prayer, Ṭarīqa Kasnazāniyya*)

Table of Contents

Ṭarīqa ʿAliyya Qādiriyya Kasnazāniyya

The Arabic word "Ṭarīqa" means "way." Technically, the term denotes the way to draw near to Allah, which He revealed to the Prophet Muḥammad (*ṣallā Allah ʿalaihi wa sallam*)[1] in the Qur'an and which the Sunna (Tradition) of the Prophet interpreted. "Ṭarīqa" as a technical term occurs in the Qur'an in the following verse: "And if they remain straight on the Ṭarīqa (Way), We will provide them water to drink in abundance" (72.16).

Ṭarīqa ʿAliyya Qādiriyya Kasnazāniyya is one of the largest Sufi Ṭarīqas in the world. It is named after three of the greatest Masters of Sufism: Imam ʿAlī bin Abī Ṭālib, Shaikh ʿAbd al-Qādir al-Gaylānī, and Shaikh ʿAbd al-Karīm Shah al-Kasnazān. The Kurdish title "Shah al-Kasnazān" means "the Sultan of the unseen." Ṭarīqa Kasnazāniyya, as it is known in brief, has an unbroken chain of Shaikhs from the Prophet (*ṣallā Allah ʿalaihi wa sallam*) to the present Master Shaikh Muḥammad al-Kasnazān (born 15/4/1938) (may Allah sanctify their secrets). Each Shaikh received the mastership of the Ṭarīqa by hand from his predecessor.

---

[1] This expression roughly means "prayer and peace from Allah be upon him." It is usually mentioned after the name or title of the Prophet, as commanded in this Qur'anic verse: "Allah and His angels sends prayer on the Prophet. O you who believe! Send prayer on him and salute him with a salutation" (33.56).

The blessed Ṭarīqa was revealed to the Prophet (*ṣallā Allah ʿalaihi wa sallam*), who passed on his spiritual knowledge to the Master of the Ṭarīqa after him, Imam ʿAlī bin Abī Ṭālib. An unbroken chain of Shaikhs continued from Imam ʿAlī through two lines. The first line, which is that of the family of the Prophet (*ṣallā Allah ʿalaihi wa sallam*), starts with Imam Ḥussein, to Imam ʿAlī Zain al-ʿĀbidīn, to Imam Muḥammad al-Bāqir, to Imam Jaʿfar al-Ṣādiq, to Imam Mūsā al-Kāẓim, and to Imam ʿAlī al-Ridhā. Imam ʿAlī handed the Ṭarīqa through its second line to Shaikh Ḥasan al-Baṣrī, to Shaikh Ḥabīb al-ʿAjamī, to Shaikh Dā'ūd aṭ-Ṭā'ī, to Shaikh Maʿrūf al-Karkhī, who was also given the mastership of the Ṭarīqa by his other Master, Imam ʿAlī al-Ridhā.

The chain of Shaikhs of Ṭarīqa Kasnazāniyya continues from Shaikh Maʿrūf al-Karkhī, to Shaikh as-Sarī as-Saqaṭī, to Shaikh Junaid al-Baghdādī, to Shaikh Abī Bakr ash-Shiblī, to Shaikh ʿAbd al-Wāḥid al-Yamānī, to Shaikh Abī Faraj aṭ-Ṭarsūsī, to Shaikh ʿAlī al-Hagārī, to Shaikh Abī Saʿīd al-Makhzūmī, to Shaikh ʿAbd al-Qādir al-Gaylānī, to Shaikh ʿAbd ar-Razzāq al-Gaylānī, to Shaikh Dā'ūd aṭḥ-Ṭḥānī, to Shaikh Muḥammad Gharībullah, to Shaikh ʿAbd al-Fattāḥ as-Sayyāḥ, to Shaikh Muḥammad Qāsim, to Shaikh Muḥammad Ṣādiq, to Shaikh Ḥussein al-Baḥrānī, to Shaikh Aḥmad al-Iḥsā'ī, to Shaikh Ismāʿīl al-Wilyānī, to Shaikh Muḥyī ad-Dīn Karkūk, to Shaikh ʿAbd aṣ-Ṣamad Gala Zarda, to Shaikh Ḥussein Qāzān Qāya, to Shaikh ʿAbd al-Qādir Qāzān Qāya, to Shaikh ʿAbd al-Karīm

Shah al-Kasnazān, to Shaikh ʿAbd al-Qādir al-Kasnazān, to Shaikh Ḥussein al-Kasnazān, to Shaikh ʿAbd al-Karīm al-Kasnazān, and to the present Master Shaikh Muḥammad al-Kasnazān.

Sayyid[2] Shaikh Muḥammad al-Kasnazān is a descendant of the Prophet (*ṣallā Allah ʿalaihi wa sallam*). He is the son of Sayyid ʿAbd al-Karīm al-Kasnazān, son of Sayyid ʿAbd al-Qādir al-Kasnazān, son of Sayyid ʿAbd al-Karīm Shah al-Kasnazān, son of Sayyid Ḥussein, son of Sayyid Ḥasan, son of Sayyid ʿAbd al-Karīm, son of Sayyid Ismāʿīl al-Wilyānī, son of Sayyid Muḥammad al-Nūdaihī, son of Sayyid Bābā ʿAlī al-Wandarīna, son of Sayyid Bābā Rasūl al-Kabīr, son of Sayyid ʿAbd al-Sayyid al-Thānī, son of Sayyid ʿAbd al-Rasūl, son of Sayyid Qalandar, son of Sayyid ʿAbd al-Sayyid, son of Sayyid ʿĪsā al-Aḥdab, son of Sayyid Ḥussein, son of Sayyid Bayazīd, son of Sayyid ʿAbd al-Karīm al-Awwal, son of Sayyid ʿĪsā al-Barazanjī, son of Sayyid Bābā ʿAlī al-Hamadānī, son of Sayyid Yūsuf al-Hamadānī (known as Shihāb ad-Dīn), son of Sayyid Muḥammad al-Manṣūr, son of Sayyid ʿAbd al-ʿAzīz, son of Sayyid ʿAbd Allah, son of Sayyid Ismāʿīl al-Muḥaddath, son of Imam Mūsā al-Kāẓim, son of Imam Jaʿfar al-Ṣādiq, son of Imam Muḥammad al-Bāqir, son of Imam ʿAlī Zain al-ʿĀbidīn, son of Imam Ḥussein, son of Imam ʿAlī bin Abī Ṭālib and Sayyida Fāṭima al-

[2] The title "Sayyid" has two different usages. It is the equivalent of "Mr" in English, but it also serves as an honorific title indicating that the person is a descendant of the Prophet Muḥammad (*ṣallā Allah ʿalaihi wa sallam*).

Zahrā' the daughter of the Messenger of Allah and the last Prophet, our Master Muḥammad (*ṣallā Allah ʿalaihi wa sallam*).

The person who wants to follow the Sufi way of Ṭarīqa Kasnazāniyya must first take the *baiʿa* (pledge or covenant). The dervish-to-be puts his hand in the hand of one of the "caliphs" and recites after them certain statements in which he declares his repentance to God and pledges to follow the Shaikhs of the Ṭarīqa. A caliph is a dervish to whom the Master has given permission to initiate people on his behalf. When a male caliph gives the pledge to a female, she is asked to hold the beads of the caliph instead of his hand. The fact that the pledge should be by hand is an application of this verse which describes how the early Muslims pledged allegiance to the Prophet (*ṣallā Allah ʿalaihi wa sallam*): "Those who pledge allegiance to you are actually pledging allegiance to Allah, Allah's hand is over their hands. Anyone who breaks his vow does so to his own detriment. As for anyone who fulfils his vow, Allah will give him a great reward" (48.10).

Ḥaḍrat[3] Shaikh Muḥammad al-Kasnazān calls the pledge the "spiritual touch," referring to its deep spiritual significance despite its simple appearance. When the dervish-to-be puts his hand in the hand of the caliph it represents putting his hand in the hand of the present Shaikh. The hand of the present Shaikh is in the hand of his predecessor, and so all Shaikhs are connected in an unbroken chain to the Prophet (*ṣallā*

---

[3] This honorific title, which is used for religious and non-religious individuals, denotes the person's elevated status. It is often used when referring to a Shaikh.

Allah ʿalaihi wa sallam). This is why pledging allegiance to the present Shaikh of the Ṭarīqa represents taking the pledge with the Prophet (*ṣallā Allah ʿalaihi wa sallam*) himself.

Spiritual development in the Ṭarīqa consists of three consecutive stations of *fanā'* that build on each other. Linguistically, "fanā'" means "vanishing," but in Sufism it denotes the disappearance of the distinct self through the extinction of one's will. The first station is fanā' in the Shaikh. Attaining this station means achieving complete obedience to the Shaikh, in which case the Shaikh becomes permanently present in the seeker's heart. The second station is fanā' in the Prophet (*ṣallā Allah ʿalaihi wa sallam*), which would then lead to the ultimate goal of the Sufi way: fanā' in Allah.

In addition to the obligatory duties of Sharīʿa, such as the daily prayers and the fasting of Ramadan, the Sufi way has further duties in the form of specific "dhikrs" (prayers of remembrance of Allah) that have great spiritual secrets. These dhikrs were revealed to the Shaikhs of Ṭarīqa Kasnazāniyya as a result of their sincere worship and total dedication to Allah. The dhikrs of the Ṭarīqa have immense benefits in cleansing the heart of the seeker of vagaries, arrogance, and all that Allah has forbidden. They help the dervish on the way of spiritual development that he has pledged to follow. They are the provision of the seeker on his journey on the Sufi way of Ṭarīqa Kasnazāniyya: "Take provision, and the best provision is piety" (2.197).

Each dhikr is performed in specific numbers. Some

are read daily at certain times, whereas others can be done at any time. Ṭarīqa Kasnazāniyya also has a dhikr that the seekers perform collectively, in which they stand in concentric circles. This dhikr is accompanied by tambourines and drums. The drum of dhikr was introduced by ḥaḍrat Shaikh ʿAbd al-Qādir al-Gaylānī, and is hence known as "the drum of al-Gaylānī."

This chapter is a short introduction to Ṭarīqa Kasnazāniyya, but the reader who is interested in more details may consult the books that have been published by the Ṭarīqa.

As a preface to the accounts of the karāmas, I next give a short introduction to the concept of "karāma" and its significance.

Karāma (Wonder)

Sufism is based on firm Qur'anic foundations that will remain until the Day of Resurrection:

- Putting the love of Allah and the Prophet (*ṣallā Allah ʿalaihi wa sallam*) above every other feeling and attachment: "Say: 'If your parents, your children, your siblings, your spouses, your kindred, money you have earned, a business you worry may slacken, and homes you cherish are dearer to you than Allah, His messenger, and striving in His cause, then wait until Allah brings His judgment.' Allah does not guide the disobedient people" (9.24); "Say: 'If you love Allah then follow me and Allah will love you and forgive your sins. Allah is forgiving, merciful'" (3.31).
- Striving against one's lower self and its evil inclinations: "But as for him who feared the station of his Lord and prohibited his soul from lust (40), paradise is the abode" (79.41).
- Unceasingly calling people to Allah using wisdom and peaceful means: "Call to the way of your Lord with wisdom and good admonition, and debate with them in the best manner. Allah knows best who stray from His way and He knows best the guided ones" (16.125).

Anybody who sincerely follows this way and meets its requirements receives all that Allah promised His good servants, including paranormal experiences. Later

Muslim scholars have differentiated between the paranormal feats that were performed or experienced by the Prophets, who are servants whom Allah elected, gave revelation to, and drew near, and those that occurred and occur to the "*Walīs*," who are servants that Allah brought close to Him. Scholars used the term "*mu'jiza* (miracle)" for any paranormal feat by a Prophet, and they coined the term "*karāma*" for any paranormal experience of a Walī.

The term "*karāma*" is derived from the verb "*karrama*," which means "to honour." It reflects the fact that such a paranormal feat "honours" the Walī for their sincere and truthful submission to Allah.

The following verses expressly state that the righteous people experience karāmas in this world:

> Those who say "Allah is our Lord" and then follow the straight path will have angels descend on them [saying]: "Do not fear and do not grieve, but have the good news of paradise, which you have been promised. (30) We are your allies in this world and the hereafter. You will have in it whatever your souls desire and you will have in it whatever you request (31) — a gift sent down from One who is forgiving, merciful." (41.32)

Allah reiterates this fact in the following verses:

> Surely, Allah's friends shall have no fear on them nor shall they grieve (62). They are those who believe and are pious (63). The shall have the good tidings in this world and in the Hereafter. There is no changing the words of Allah. That is the great triumph. (10.64)

The Prophet (*ṣallā Allah 'alaihi wa sallam*) has also

reported the following Qudsī speech[4] that shows how Allah honours the Walīs with paranormal feats:

> I declare war against the person who shows hostility to a Walī of Mine. The most beloved things with which My servant comes nearer to Me, is what I have enjoined upon him. My servant keeps on coming closer to Me through performing supererogatory acts of worship till I love him. When I love him I become his sense of hearing with which he hears, his sense of sight with which he sees, his hand with which he grips, and his leg with which he walks. If he asks Me for something, I give him, and if he asks for My refuge (against something), I give him My refuge.[5]

But karāmas are never what the seeker targets; what they seek is nearness to Allah. Karāmas are one fruit and proof that the person is on the way to Allah.

One significant difference between the muʿjiza and the karāma is that the Prophet is always commanded to talk about his miracles and publicise them: "As for the grace of your Lord, talk about it" (93.11). Karāmas, on the other hand, are divided into two groups, one that must be concealed and another that must be publicised. The former includes paranormal experiences that the seeker has during his worship, sleep, or daily life. Allah grants these karāmas to the servant to strengthen his faith, reassure his heart, and delight him. Being personal gifts to the worshipper, these karāmas, ḥaḍrat Shaikh

---

[4] The Qudsī speeches are revelations from Allah to the Prophet (*ṣallā Allah ʿalaihi wa sallam*) but they are not part of the Qur'anic revelation.

[5] Al-Bukhārī, Muḥammad, *al-Jāmiʿ al-Ṣaḥīḥ lil-Bukhārī*, Vol. 3, no. 6273, p. 493, Riyadh, 2008.

Muḥammad al-Kasnazān stresses, must be kept secret by the dervish; they may share them only with their Shaikh.

The second type of karāma is granted in the context of calling people to the way of Allah. Accordingly, like the miracles of the Prophets, these karāmas should be publicised as reminders for people. All the karāmas in this book are of this exhortative type, hence they are being made public.

Introduction

This book compiles a very small number of paranormal feats that Allah has gifted to the Shaikhs of Ṭarīqa ʿAliyya Qādiriyya Kasnazāniyya and its present Master Sayyid Shaikh Muḥammad al-Kasnazān, the head of Ṭarīqa Kasnazāniyya. These karāmas were witnessed by or involved the deputy of ḥaḍrat Shaikh Muḥammad in India during his preaching tours of that country in 2011-2015. When ḥaḍrat Shaikh Muḥammad sends any of the caliphs of the Ṭarīqa to call people to Allah, he informs him that the blessings of the Shaikhs of the Ṭarīqa, which stem from the blessings of the Prophet (*ṣallā Allah ʿalaihi wa sallam*), will accompany him in the form of karāmas. These karāmas confirm to people the truthfulness of the preaching and that Ṭarīqa Kasnazāniyya indeed represents a spiritual link with the Prophet (*ṣallā Allah ʿalaihi wa sallam*).

I have compiled fifty-five karāma reports. Some of the individual reports include more than one karāma. For instance, one report documents the healing of over two hundred patients with dengue fever.[6] Furthermore, many

[6] This is a mosquito-borne disease caused by the dengue virus. It is found in tropical and sub-tropical regions, including India. Symptoms include fever, headaches, muscle and joint pains, and skin rashes. In a small proportion of cases the disease develops into the life-threatening "severe dengue" fever. I have referred to all cases in this book as "dengue" and have not attempted to identify cases of "sever dengue" because the caliph did not check the medical reports of the patients before he treated them. Nevertheless, the symptoms of

of these karāmas include more than one paranormal feat. For example, in one karāma, a boy with dengue fever was cured by drinking water over which the caliph had read a special dhikr that ḥaḍrat Shaikh Muḥammad al-Kasnazān had given him permission to use. But the caliph was in the city of Sulaymaniyah in the north of Iraq, while the glass of water was in Kausar Nagar in the city of Bangalore in India. The distance between the two cities is over four thousand kilometres. The third paranormal feat in this karāma is that the water started to boil as the caliph started to read the prayer.

Some karāmas are simple, although of course still paranormal, such as the healing of a patient after taking the pledge of the Ṭarīqa. Others are more sophisticated, with their details unfolding over weeks. One such example is the karāma in which the caliph saw in repeated dreams phone messages instructing him to go to a place that was unknown to him.

I have classified the karāmas in different categories according to the main aspect of paranormality in each karāma. I have put each category into a separate chapter. For instance, all karāmas that include paranormal healing have been collected in one chapter. No karāma was included in more than one chapter, even if it contains more than one paranormal aspect, to avoid repetition. To facilitate referring to any karāma specifically, I have given each a title that indicates the main paranormal feat it involves.

---

many cases suggested advanced stages of the disease.

The narrator in all karāmas is the caliph who witnessed them. The edited text is based on the narratives I compiled from the written diaries of the caliph in India and telephone and face-to-face interviews I conducted with the caliph to clarify certain details. I have also interviewed some witnesses of the karāmas by phone.

It is worth noting that the caliph communicated on a daily basis to ḥaḍrat Shaikh Muḥammad al-Kasnazān the details of his preaching tours. He would mention to the Shaikh any karāmas he witnessed. This is why there are sometimes comments by the Shaikh on some of the karāmas.

For consistency in documenting the karāmas, I have mentioned the date and location of each karāma before its account. In most cases, the day, month, and year have been listed, as these dates were taken from the caliph's diaries. In some cases, the exact date of the karāma is unknown. This is usually due to the fact that the exact date is not written in the diaries, but at times because of the unavailability of written accounts of these karāmas. In these cases, the details came only from interviews that took place a relatively a long time after the karāmas themselves. When mentioning the location, I tried to name the city and the state. The precise locations of some karāmas could not be identified, because they took place in small villages that are not mentioned in the diaries, as they are unknown or the caliph could not remember.

The caliph has documented some of the karāmas

using photos and films. At times, he took photos of those who experienced the karāmas. At others, he filmed the individuals concerned talking about what happened to them.

I have added footnotes to explain terms and concepts that some readers might be unfamiliar with. I have also compiled them in a glossary at the end of the book for easy reference.

1

Paranormal Healing

This chapter covers cases of paranormal healing, i.e. healing that could not have happened naturally or by mere human intervention. In some of these cases, the blessings of the Shaikhs of the Ṭarīqa cured illnesses that doctors had given up on, cured others instantly, or cured without surgery some that would normally require surgical intervention, and other aspects of paranormal healing.

Dying Little Girl

Date: 2012
Location: Kaveripattinam - Krishnagiri - Tamil Nadu

I saw in a dream ḥaḍrat Shaikh Muḥammad al-Kasnazān introduce a five- or six-year-old girl to me. He said: "Son, take care of her!" I did not pay much attention to the dream but it remained on my mind. After two or three weeks, I saw the Shaikh with the girl for the second time. This time he said: "Her name is Mariam; take care of her." After the second dream, I started to ask whenever I went out preaching whether any person in the audience had a girl called Mariam who may be in need of treatment. After about one and a half months, the dream recurred for the third time. This time the Shaikh said: "Mariam is ill; read the so-and-so dhikr seventy times."

At this point, I decided to inform the Shaikh. I told him that I have seen a dream three times in around two months in which he informed me of a sick Mariam and instructed me to pray for her using that dhikr seventy times. The Shaikh said: "Offer this dhikr to your Shaikhs first. Mariam is on her way to you." I continued to ask in every preaching journey, before I started speaking, whether any one in the audience had a daughter called "Mariam."

One day I was on a preaching tour and, as usual, before I started speaking, I asked about the girl. I repeated the question two or three times, at which point a tall brown woman stood up and said she had a daughter called "Sanā Mariam." This family is related to the people in whose house we were. When I asked about her, the mother said that the girl had been ill for three months. She did not know what was wrong with the child, but she had a high fever. She had taken her to several doctors, including some in Bangalore, but they could not diagnose her illness. The girl was so ill that her mother had been putting drops of water in her mouth and had laid her in the direction of the qibla in Mecca expecting her to die. I asked her to bring the girl. They lived two or three houses away from the house in which I was speaking.

Mariam bore similarities in age and looks to the girl I saw in the dreams. When I put her on my lap her body felt as hot as a stove, so much so that I started sweating.

I asked for water in an unused container. Mariam's family gave me a bowl that they had brought from Medina and put water in it. I recited the dhikr of the Shaikh seventy times over the water while Mariam was on my lap. I then helped her drink the water. I told the people: "She will sleep, so put her in another room."

I then started my preaching speech which lasted for about an hour. After I finished, forty five people took the pledge, then the landlord invited us for lunch. As soon as we went to have lunch, Mariam came running like a homing pigeon, threw herself on me, and started eating with us. As a result of this karāma, another twenty five to thirty people took the pledge. When I informed the Shaikh about what happened, he said: "If three people witness an event it is considered "successive" (*mutawātir*),[7] yet this was seen by sixty!" He added: "This may not necessarily have an impact now but will do in the future."

I have taken several photos of Mariam: when she was ill on my lap, when she started eating, and when she had fully recovered.

---

[7] The term "successive" (*mutawātir*) was coined by Muslim scholars to describe any report that was witnessed by several reliable witnesses. For instance, all of the Qur'anic text is considered to be "successive" because every verse was transmitted by a number of Companions of the Prophet (*ṣallā Allah ʿalaihi wa sallam*), whereas not all Prophetic traditions are successive.

Woman in Need of Nasal Surgery

Date: 19/10/2012

Location: Bangarapet - Karnataka

About a week ago, I was in a very poor village when a woman came to me crying and said:

> I have a pain in my nose. The doctors say that it requires an operation that costs thirty thousand rupees, yet I can hardly get by and my husband is unemployed.

I gave her the pledge. Today she came back looking very happy and told me this:

> I saw in a dream the Shaikh replacing my nose with another. When I woke up, I found drops of blood and snot on my nose and on the pillow. I am now very well.

She went to her doctor and told him that she has been healed. The doctor asked her if she received treatment from other doctors, which she denied. He asked her about what happened, and she told him that he may or may not believe her. He still wanted to know. She told him something along these lines:

> I took the pledge of the Ṭarīqa from a man who had come from Baghdad and is a caliph of a Shaikh. The Shaikh visited me in my dream and performed an operation in which he cut off and replaced my nose.

The doctor argued that this is unbelievable because it is mythical, whereas medicine is based on science. The woman replied:

> This is what happened. The paranormal nature of my healing is confirmed by the fact that the last x-ray of my nose was taken only four days ago. You asked me to come back to see you after you gave me drops for

my nose. You also know that my nose has been blocked by a bone from birth.

I asked her if she had seen a photo of ḥaḍrat Shaikh Muḥammad al-Kasnazān to which she answered in the negative. When I showed her his photo, she jumped at it and started kissing it. She confirmed that it was him who healed her in her dream. I asked her about the language in which the Shaikh spoke to her, and she said it was Urdu.

I have taken photos of the woman and also filmed my conversation with her. I have x-rays from both before and after the healing.

Woman with Gynaecological Illness

Date: 20/10/2012

Location: Kaveripattinam - Krishnagiri - Tamil Nadu

A week ago, a woman came to see me with her mother. She suffered from a very long monthly period that would last twenty days. She had seen a large number of doctors, some of whom advised that she should have her ovaries removed to avoid getting cancer. I gave her and her mother the pledge, asked her to do the dhikrs of the Ṭarīqa, and reminded her to remain modest, as is required of every Muslim woman. Today she came back to see me looking very happy. The bleeding had stopped and she is now asking that her period becomes regular by the blessings of dhikr. She said:

After visiting you, I saw in a dream a man who told me: "I am Abū Sa'īd. This is the deputy of Shaikh Muḥammad al-Kasnazān. He has connected your heart to the heart of Shaikh Muḥammad and the Greatest Ghawth.[8] You do not need an operation. You will be alright."

When the Shaikh heard about this karāma, he said that the man in the dream was ḥaḍrat Shaikh Abū Sa'īd al-Makhzūmī.[9]

Crying Sick Child

Date: 3/11/2012
Location: Saraipalya - Bangalore - Karnataka

I gave the pledge on the land of the takya[10] to eighteen people, including a woman who was carrying

---

[8] The Arabic word "Ghawth" refers to a top spiritual rank. The word means "helper," in reference to the fact that a "Ghawth" is someone who has spiritual powers that allow him to paranormally help others. "Al-Ghawth al-A'ẓam" or "the Greatest Ghawth" is a title that Allah vested on Shaikh 'Abd al-Qādir al-Gaylānī, signifying the fact that he is the greatest of all Ghawths.

[9] Shaikh Abū Sa'īd al-Makhzūmī is the Master whom Shaikh 'Abd al-Qādir al-Gaylānī took the pledge from and succeeded as the Master of the Ṭarīqa.

[10] "Takya" is the place of worship of the Ṭarīqa. The Kurdish origin of this term is the two words "tak kah" which mean "one" and "place," respectively. "Takya" then means "the place of practicing the oneness of God." Other common names for "takya" include "khāniqāh" and "zāwiya." I have used the expression "land of the takya" to refer to the place of the takya in Bangalore before it was built, as it was only a fenced piece of land. The building of the takya started at the end of 2013.

her sick one-year-old child. He had stopped suckling for two days and would not stop crying. I gave him water after reading over it what my Shaikh had taught me. He was immediately cured.

Man with Dengue Fever

Date: 4/11/2012

Location: Saraipalya - Bangalore - Karnataka

I gave the pledge on the land of the takya to sixteen people, one of whom had dengue fever and was healed immediately. I said to the caliphs: "This is by virtue of the spiritual power of the Shaikhs. It is they who cure all illnesses."

Man Who Was Punished with Blindness Sees Again

Date: 5/12/2012

Location: Saraipalya - Bangalore - Karnataka

A blind man came to me and told me the following:

> I said bad things about Shaikh Muḥammad al-Kasnazān, and went to bed while thinking of that. In the dream a man came to me, stretched out his hand, and said: "Give me your vision." I said: "How can I give you my vision?" He clenched his fist, so I woke up scared, and discovered that I had lost my sight.

The blind man described the man who took his sight. He resembled ḥaḍrat Shaikh Muḥammad al-Kasnazān. He also said that the Shaikh spoke to him in his language. I told the man: "I will give you the pledge, and Allah willing, the Shaikh will not turn down my request. You must consider this proof." He replied: "I repent to Allah. I am someone who prays, so I am not a disbeliever, but I insulted one of the Walīs of Allah. I repent to Allah now." I mentioned to him the saying of the Prophet (*ṣallā Allah ʿalaihi wa sallam*) in which he declares that Allah's enemies are those who steal the property of the orphans and those who show enmity to Allah's Walīs. The man repeated his repentance. I recited a dhikr that the Shaikh had given me permission to use over water. Glory be to Allah, I have found this dhikr to be useful for curing various illnesses and solving all kinds of problems. I asked him to put drops of the water in his eyes. I also gave him my head cover to wrap around his eyes, while I was asking for *madad*[11] from the Shaikh.

I asked the man to sleep. When he woke up after an hour, he could see a little light. I left him and went to another village, where I gave the pledge to twenty-one people. After returning at sunset, the blind man came to me, having had his vision restored by the favour of the Shaikh. He made me and those present cry by what he had to say. He thanked the Shaikh for giving him back

---

[11] The Arabic term *madad* means "help" or "support." In Sufism, it refers to the paranormal help and intervention of the Shaikh of the Ṭarīqa using the spiritual powers that Allah gave him. This technical use of the term is of Qur'anic origin: "When you [O you who believe!] asked your Lord for help, so He responded to you [saying]: 'I am *mumiddukum* (giving you the *madad*) of one thousand angels in succession'" (8.9).

his sight.

Over Two Hundred Dengue Fever Patients

Date: 5/11/2012
Location: Bangalore - Karnataka

Less than two weeks ago, I sent a caliph to give the pledge to a woman who was ill in hospital with dengue fever. I also gave him water for the patient to drink, after I read over it the special dhikr that the Shaikh had allowed me to use. Ten days later, the woman came to see me, having fully recovered, and kissed where my foot stood. She said she will go for 'Umra (the lesser pilgrimage to Mecca) to fulfil a vow she made for her recovery. I recorded an interview with her in which she discussed her recovery.

We then published details of this karāma on YouTube, including photos of the woman in hospital taking the pledge and after she recovered. We mentioned that Ṭarīqa Kasnazāniyya promises to treat anyone who has dengue fever, provided they take the pledge. This is not confined to Muslims but also to non-Muslims who are willing to take the pledge and embrace Islam. We published the address to contact us. As a result, we successfully treated two hundred and ten people with the disease.

Man with Crippling Illness

Date: 20/11/2012

Location: Sudama Nagar - Bangalore - Karnataka

A man with a drip in his arm and carried by two men came to visit me. He was in pain and could not walk. The doctors could not diagnose his illness, but there was a possibility that that it was the beginning of dengue fever. As he was approaching me, his face looked to me like a pig's face and his body looked full of worms. I instructed him to sit away from me, and then I asked him: "How many times have you prayed in your life?" The man replied: "I perform the Friday prayer every other week, and I do my daily prayer when I am in need." At this point, the two men who brought him stood up and said to him: "Then you have been deceiving us all this time, claiming that you have performed the pilgrimage to Allah's House?" His lies were exposed. He said: "By Allah, I do not know what happened." I said to him: "Repent to Allah," so he said: "There is no God save Allah." I gave him the pledge, and he immediately stood up on his own and cried a lot.

Man with Facial Allergic Reaction

Date: 7/12/2012

Location: Saraipalya - Bangalore - Karnataka

About ten days ago, I gave the pledge on the land of the takya to a young man who was suffering from an allergic reaction in the face because of his long-term use of varnish in his job as a wood painter. I told him that I would give him water that he should wash his face with. I asked for madad from the Shaikh over the water and gave it to him. He came to me today in a very happy mood and said:

> I have seen Shaikh Muḥammad al-Kasnazān in my sleep. He used a spray on my face and said: "You will have no problem after today." I swear by Allah that my face recovered from that day.

Injured Hand

Date: 31/12/2012

Location: Saraipalya - Bangalore - Karnataka

A Hindu man came to see me. His injured left hand was causing him a lot of pain. He said: "I will donate this money with my left hand, and if it heals then I will donate more and take the pledge." I gave him the pledge and he made a two thousand rupees donation to the takya with his injured hand. As soon as he moved his hand back after handing the money to me, it fully recovered. He then donated another three thousand rupees with his right hand and embraced Islam.

Man with Jaw Cancer

Date: 8/9/2013

Location: Kausar Nagar - Bangalore - Karnataka

A few days ago, someone suffering from jaw cancer came to me. I gave him the pledge and sand from the shrine of ḥaḍrat Shaikh ʿAbd al-Karīm Shah al-Kasnazān. I asked him to mix the sand with water and use it as a gargle and come back after a week. Ḥaḍrat Shaikh Muḥammad al-Kasnazān had told me that the blessing of this sand makes it suitable to treat any illness. I did not have the opportunity to see the patient again, as he lives elsewhere, but I heard that he recovered. As I did not see him again, I could not record an interview with him.

Man with Kidney Failure

Date: 28/9/2013
Location: Tumkur - Karnataka

A man came to me and said: "I will not leave this door until you promise me that I will be cured of my disease." One of his kidneys had failed and both of his legs down to the feet were swollen. I found myself in a state I could not understand, but I cried a lot and begged ḥaḍrat Shaikh Muḥammad al-Kasnazān. I said to the man: "You will be cured, Allah willing, by the blessing of the Shaikh." The man had been told by the doctors not to drink more than one glass of water a day, but I gave him a one-litre bottle of water, asked him to drink it, and told him that I will still be in town the following day. I gave him the pledge and told him to ask for madad from the Shaikh. He came the following day and said: "By Allah, this Shaikh is great..." He paused, asked Allah for forgiveness, and then continued saying: "Had the Messenger of Allah not said 'there will be no Prophet after me' I would have said that this Shaikh (meaning Shaikh Muḥammad al-Kasnazān) is the Prophet of this nation." He then told me about what happened. After he arrived home, the water that I had given him to drink started to have an effect. He went to the toilet and passed water after not being able to urinate for three weeks in a row.

Boy with Dengue Fever

Date: 2014

Location: Sulaymaniyah - Iraq / Kausar Nagar - Bangalore - Karnataka

I was in Sulaymaniyah to have a hernia operation when dervishes from Kausar Nagar in the city of Bangalore in India rang me. The distance between Sulaymaniyah and Bangalore is over four thousand kilometres. They told me about a boy who had dengue fever, who was in the Apollo hospital, and asked me to pray for him using the dhikr that the Shaikh had granted me permission to read. I asked them to prepare a glass of water and put the mobile phone on top of the glass. I asked them to turn on the speakerphone because I was going to say "hello" to let them know when I had finished reciting the dhikr, so that we could speak afterwards. After I finished the dhikr the dervishes told me that the water started to boil when I was reciting the dhikr. I asked them to give the water to the patient to drink and, Allah willing, he will recover. After one day, the boy fully recovered and left hospital.

Girl with Chikungunya Fever

Date: 2014
Location: Bangalore – Karnataka

I was visited by a girl who had previously had chikungunya.[12] Symptoms of this disease include high fever, joint pain, and rash. The doctor had told her that all the symptoms would go away when she recovered. But while the fever and joint pain had disappeared, the rash was still there after three months. One of the dervishes of the Ṭarīqa, whose name is Fairūz, advised the girl to see me about her illness.

When I saw her, I introduced myself as a caliph of ḥaḍrat Shaikh Muḥammad al-Kasnazān. I also told her that all that I could do for her was to give her the pledge and teach her about the dhikrs of the Ṭarīqa, and, God willing, she would be cured by the spiritual power of the Shaikh. I read over water a dhikr that the Shaikh had taught me and gave the water to her. I also gave her another quantity of water into which I mixed sand from the shrine of ḥaḍrat Shaikh ʿAbd al-Karīm Shah al-Kasnazān. I asked her to collect the water after she washed her body with it and to throw it in a garden or a clean body of water, in order to properly dispose of the pure sand.

Two weeks later, this dervish came back to tell me

[12] Chikungunya is a viral disease transmitted to humans by infected mosquitoes.

that she had been totally cured of the rash and that her skin was back to normal due to the blessings of the Ṭarīqa. I have filmed her talking about this karāma.

Man with Facial Paralysis

Date: 23/11/2014

Location: Saraipalya - Bangalore - Karnataka

A dervish who had taken the pledge of Ṭarīqa Kasnazāniyya several years before my arrival in India came to the takya. He recounted the following karāma which occurred to him in either 2005 or 2006:

> I had a stroke about sixteen or seventeen years ago. At the time, an English doctor treated me, and I achieved eighty per cent recovery. I was left with partial paralysis of the face, as my mouth remained permanently twisted toward the right side. This prevented me from speaking properly. For example, I could not pronounce the letter "f."
>
> Sometime after taking the pledge of the Ṭarīqa, I went to work in Saudi Arabia. One day, after performing the dawn prayer, I stood in front of a photo of Shaikh Muḥammad al-Kasnazān to talk to him directly, and said to him: "In the past, I did not pray and used to talk nonsense and say anything, even if it was not good. Nevertheless, before my stroke, I did not have any problem with my mouth and used to speak fluently. Yet, I am now a practicing dervish, observing the prayer and dhikrs, but I cannot pronounce words properly; why are you not helping me?" I was talking with some anger.
>
> When I slept that night, I had a strange dream. I was in a hospital that was unfamiliar to me. There was a doctor who had come from China. He was wearing a

> surgical face mask. He said to me that he was going to cure my facial paralysis. I lay in bed and the doctor started treating me with acupuncture. The treatment lasted about half an hour, during which time he inserted needles into various parts of my body. When he finished, the doctor said to me: "Your treatment is now complete. You are ninety-eight per cent cured." I asked him: "Sir, who are you?" He then removed his facial mask, and I realized that it was Shaikh Muḥammad al-Kasnazān.
>
> I woke up scared. It was about three o'clock in the morning. I performed my ablutions and the dawn prayer. I then looked into the mirror and saw that my facial paralysis had completely gone away. My mouth was now normal. The other two per cent that the Shaikh mentioned in the dream concerns a little issue I still have at times when I swallow food and I am not careful. All I need in such cases is a drink of water.

I have filmed this dervish describe his illness and the karāma that healed him.

2

Fulfilled Dreams about Taking the Pledge

In each of these karāmas, a person saw a dream or more than one dream in which he was instructed or learned that he was going to take the pledge of the Ṭarīqa. The dream later came true.

Instruction by Shaikh ʿAbd al-Qādir al-Gaylānī on Taking the Pledge

Date: 12/10/2012

Location: Saraipalya - Bangalore - Karnataka

I went to the land of the takya in the company of two people, a driver and a dervish who helped me with my needs. I sat looking at the place and thinking: "O Shaikh Muḥammad! I am sad today, and I do not know why. Deep sorrow has set in on my heart. Every day I hear news that hurts my heart. Now I am on your land, in your takya, so do you accept that I am alone?" I was thinking of what I was going to tell the Shaikh about preaching that day as not much had happened.

Less than ten minutes had passed when ten men and ten women came. They greeted me and sat down. I asked them about their needs. They replied: "We have agreed to come to the land of ḥaḍrat Shaikh ʿAbd al-Qādir al-

Gaylānī and ask for needs we have to be fulfilled. Each one of us has a need, and you are the servant of this place, so tell us what to do." I gave them all the pledge and the dhikrs. Then one of them said:

> A week ago I saw in a dream a man talking to me about a pledge and repentance[13] but I did not know what he meant. I said: "Sir, please explain." He said: "Go and take the pledge." I said: "Who are you?" He replied: "I am the Greatest Ghawth." Now I know the meaning of the pledge, which is to dedicate myself to Allah and pledge that to Him.

He was then overcome by crying.

Repeated Instruction by Shaikh ʿAbd al-Qādir al-Gaylānī on Taking the Pledge

Date: 14/10/2012

Location: Kolar - Karnataka

I went to a village seventy kilometres from Bangalore and then to another village where I gave the pledge to forty-five people. Among them there was a man who recounted the following:

> I have seen our Master al-Gaylānī in my dreams three times. Every time he would say: "Join my family," I would reply: "How do I do that, O my Master, the Greatest Ghawth?" He would reply: "Give me your hand."[14] I would then wake up. When you said today:

---

[13] The practice of taking the pledge of Ṭarīqa Kasnazāniyya involves a declaration of repentance.

[14] As mentioned earlier, taking the pledge of Ṭarīqa Kasnazāniyya is by putting the hand of the person seeking to take the pledge in the hand of the caliph.

"Give me your hand" and then I started reciting the pledge, I remembered the dream. I felt reassured that this was indeed the way of al-Gaylānī.

Prognostic Dream about Taking the Pledge

Date: 25/10/2012

Location: Saraipalya - Bangalore - Karnataka

I was visited by a poor Muslim man who sells coconut water. After exchanging greetings, he asked me: "Why are you sitting here?" I replied: "This is my house, so it is me who should ask you about what has brought you here!" He smiled and said: "You are wise." I returned the compliment: "It is rather you who are generous." The man then brought four or five coconuts from his trolley, prepared them for drinking, and gave me one and the others to dervishes that were with me. I then invited him to take the pledge, at which point he said: "I swear by Allah, I swear by Allah, I swear by Allah, this is exactly what happened in a dream I saw three days ago." This surprised me, so I asked him about his vision:

> I came to this place and saw a man who looked like you sitting here. He was wearing a green cloth similar to yours. He asked me to come forward and take the pledge. I gave him an amount of money for the sacrifice of the Eid. So here I am coming to give you fifteen thousand rupees and take the pledge.

Prognostic Dream about Taking the Pledge

Date: 1/12/2013

Location: Sudhapur – Bangalore - Karnataka

I gave the pledge to fifty-one people, including some whose Shaikh had died. When I asked one of them if he wanted to take the pledge, this is what he said:

> By Allah, for a year now I have been asking everyday Shaikh ʿAbd al-Qādir al-Gaylānī that I take a Qādirī[15] pledge from a Ghawth or a deputy of a Ghawth. I used to think that my previous Shaikh was one of the Poles (Quṭbs).[16] I have seen blessings from him, even if little, but they are nevertheless blessings as he was a caliph of a Qādirī Ṭarīqa and my Shaikh and guide. One week ago I saw in a dream that I took the pledge from a man who came from Baghdad. But I forgot the dream. When I heard of your visit, I came to see you. When I saw you I remembered the dream and thought: "If he offers me the pledge, I will take it." So here I am, having come to you and having taken the pledge from you. Allah willing, it will be the last pledge.

---

[15] The term "Qādirī" means related to Shaikh ʿAbd al-Qādir al-Gaylānī. A "Qādirī pledge" means the pledge of a Ṭarīqa whose chain of Shaikhs goes back to Shaikh ʿAbd al-Qādir.

[16] The "Quṭb," which literally means "Pole" is a very high spiritual station in Sufism.

3

Revelation of Hidden Information

This chapter consists of karāmas in which the Shaikhs of the Ṭarīqa paranormally revealed to the caliph information he could not otherwise have known. The occurrence of the revelation and its timing are not under the control of the caliph, but are the prerogative of the Shaikhs of the Ṭarīqa.

Dervish's Wish

Date: 17/10/2012

Location: Kausar Nagar – Bangalore - Karnataka

I went out on a preaching journey in which I gave the pledge to fifteen people. After returning home, I found a man of around eighty years old waiting for me. He had a very long beard and carried a staff. I greeted him and went into my house, but he followed me. He said in Urdu: "I am a Shaikh from Ṭarīqa Qādiriyya Chishtiyya, and I am a caliph of Ṭarīqa Suhrwardiyya. I have come to you because I have heard you have things we do not have. One of the caliphs of our Ṭarīqa Suhrwardiyya has taken the pledge from you and is now following you, so I came to know what made him join you and leave us." I said: "We have the Qur'an and the Sunna (Tradition) of the Prophet (*ṣallā Allah ʿalaihi wa sallam*), which you also have." He said: "True." I said: "We have dhikrs, and you have dhikrs." He said: "True." I then went on to say: "We have the Ghawth of all creatures, Quṭb al-Irshād (the Pole of Preaching),[17] and the only heir of the family of the Prophet (*ṣallā Allah ʿalaihi wa sallam*) and Shaikh ʿAbd al-Qādir al-Gaylānī, which you do not have." He said: "What proof do you have?" I replied: "Anyone who makes an untrue claim is a liar; do you have proof on what you claim about your Shaikh, before I present you with the proof of my claim?" He said: "I do not know." I said: "How come that you do not know whether your Shaikh is a Ghawth or not? Take, for example, any college or university. If it has a proper curriculum and good lecturers, you would consider it to be a credible educational institute; otherwise, you would not take notice of it." He said: "That is all true." I then went on to say: "I will now give you the proof. Have we met before?" He said: "No." I said: "Do I know you?" He said: "No." I said: "My Master, the only Ghawth in this world, has just told me that you want green beads from the shrine of al-Gaylānī, and here they are." Every time I visit India, I bring with me hundreds of beads which I have taken to the shrine of ḥaḍrat Shaikh ʿAbd al-Qādir al-Gaylānī to bless them. The man cried and I cried with him. He said: "The dervish of Ṭarīqa Suhrwardiyya was right in taking your pledge and following you, and I would also now like to take the pledge."

---

[17] "Quṭb al-Irshād" is a very high spiritual position that is occupied by one Shaikh at any point in time.

Fatal Magic

Date: 8/12/2012

Location: Tamil Nadu

I decided to go to preach in a certain village, but before going there, my chest was so strained that I could hardly breathe, although I had not stopped performing the dhikrs and invocations of madad that the Shaikh had instructed me to. I even considered postponing the trip to the village. I and all twenty-two men with me were in the middle of a spiritual exercise. I said to the person who prepares the food for our visit that I would only have bread and cucumber because I was coming to preach, not to enjoy food.

When I arrived, they brought a wreath of flowers to put on my head, but the wreath appeared to me like a large snake. I felt apprehensive, and spontaneously asked loudly for madad saying "O Shaikh Muḥammad!", and I threw the flowers on the floor. Numerous small worms, each with a white body and a black head, came out of the wreath. The scene scared all those present. I asked for the place to be hoovered to clean it so that we could start the preaching. I did not give the wreath issue any more attention. I gave the pledge to twenty-eight people, including two Hindus, and then returned home.

The person who organized the gathering later rang me to say that he would like to visit me the following day accompanied by a man who had something to tell me. I welcomed their visit. But he called again and said: "Caliph, I cannot wait until tomorrow. The man who would like to visit you had performed black magic on the flowers to kill you on the spot. But the magic has turned against him, as he has become a believer. He would like to come and show repentance in front of you, so that you forgive him." I said: "Allah forgives all sins" (39.53). The people who were with me wanted me to ask him about who asked him to do the magic, but I told them that Allah forgives what happened and that the matter was now closed. The man came indeed. He turned out to be a Hindu, so he embraced Islam. I later heard that it was a group of Salafis[18] who had become aware of my planned visit and had asked him to prepare the magic.

Women Who Had Abandoned the Prayer

Date: 2/1/2013
Location: Tamil Nadu

I went to an area that was largely Muslim, but its people had a poor understanding and practice of Islam. I gathered people in the house of one of the dervishes. Twelve veiled women came to see me. I felt uncomfortable so I asked for madad from the Shaikh. After the sermon, I said to them: "My sisters, which one of you is the most truthful?" There was no reply. I said: "If I mentioned to you a fact would you believe it?"

---

[18] The term "Salafi" is supposed to refer to a person who follows the example of the early generations of Muslims, but in reality it denotes someone who advocates an unhistorical narrow interpretation of Islam.

They replied in the affirmative. I said: "Without a sense of embarrassment?" They confirmed again. I said to those present:

> O brothers, be witnesses on this! These women, with the exception of the following two have never prayed before. One of the two women has now abandoned the prayer for a reason she knows.

All the women lowered their heads. Someone then asked them: "Is what the caliph says true?" The women answered in the affirmative. One of the two said:

> I am the one who abandoned the prayer a few days ago for a certain reason. I promise Allah that I will repent at the hand of this man.

All twelve women took the pledge, in addition to nine of the men who were present.

Impure Person

Date: 11/9/2013

Location: Kausar Nagar - Bangalore - Karnataka

Caliph Rafīq Ahmad, who is one of the active dervishes, contacted me to say that he was bringing two Muslim men who wanted to take the pledge. I waited for them in the house of caliph ʿAbd al-Bashīr, where I live on the upper floor. Suddenly, while I was sitting, ḥaḍrat Shaikh Muḥammad al-Kasnazān let me see that one of the two men was filthy. I stood up and said loudly: "Rafīq Ahmad, this man is filthy, so why do you bring him to me? Take him away from me." I then sat down. This was witnessed by caliph ʿAbd al-Bashīr and caliph

Jaʿfar.

When caliph Rafīq arrived, there was only one man, called Muḥammad Naṣīr, with him. I asked my two companions to ask him about the other person. Rafīq replied:

> As we were about to get into the rickshaw, the other person suddenly said: "I am filthy, I am filthy. I cannot go with you in case the Shaikh (meaning me) will expose me."

Caliph Jaʿfar was shaken by what he had just heard and said: "The caliph, the deputy of the Shaikh, stood up about one hour ago and said loudly: 'Rafīq Ahmad, this man is filthy, so why do you bring him to me?'" The man who came with Rafīq was astonished and said: "I had doubts about the story of our master ʿUmar with Sāriya,[19] but I believe it now. I will take the pledge from this man." He kissed my hand and foot and took the pledge.

---

[19] Sāriya was the leader of a Muslim army. One day he was in battle in Persia when his army was in the process of being surrounded by the enemy. At the same time, caliph ʿUmar bin al-Khaṭṭāb was delivering the sermon of the Friday prayer in Medina. He suddenly interrupted his sermon to shout: "Sāriya take to the mountain, take to the mountain!" He did not know why he said that. When Sāriya came back from battle he told people that when his army was being surrounded, he heard a voice saying: "Sāriya take to the mountain, take to the mountain!" He and his soldiers moved to the foot of the mountain and used it to protect the back of the army. This manoeuvre did indeed help them defeat the enemies.

Man Pretending to be a Shaikh

Date: 27/11/2013
Location: Raichur - Karnataka

After preaching to a gathering, a person called Kalīmullah Khan came to me with a disabled person. I felt uncomfortable as soon as I saw him, so I started asking for madad from ḥaḍrat Shaikh Muḥammad al-Kasnazān. He asked in Arabic about my name, so I answered: "ʿImād ad-Ddīn, a caliph of Shaikh Muḥammad al-Kasnazān." He then showed me his ID. He was a retired sergeant who currently ran a large property agency in Raichur, but was originally from Chennai. He also said that he was a member of a national committee. He said: "I have heard about you, so I came as I have some questions." I said: "Sure, please ask." He first asked: "What does the word 'Kasnazān' mean?" which I answered. Then he asked me about the origin of our Ṭarīqa and why I had come to preach to the Muslims. I told him that I do not target Muslims in particular but that this area has a lot of Muslims, and also that a lot of Hindus have also embraced Islam. I told him that he can ask my companion. As it happened, one Hindu man had embraced Islam just an hour earlier. He was surprised.

He went on to ask: "Do you have a tree?" He meant by that the family tree and the chain of Shaikhs. I gave him a printout of the chain, so he asked me: "Is your name in the chain of the Ṭarīqa?" I said: "Of course not." He then produced a printout of a chain. It turned out that he was one of the caliphs of Ṭarīqa Qādiriyya Chishtiyya. His name was there as one of the caliphs of Shaikh Nāṣir al-Qādirī al-Baghdādī. I said: "You are a caliph, not a Shaikh." He protested: "I am a Shaikh." I said: "I am a servant of the Ṭarīqa and a servant of ḥaḍrat Shaikh Muḥammad al-Kasnazān." He asked me a lot of questions.

I then said to him: "You have asked me many questions, but I would like to ask you one question." I had a feeling of annoyance that I could not describe. I actually had no particular question in mind, but I stood up and said in a somewhat loud and hoarse voice:

> What is the meaning of the following verse that is said by Ibrahim (peace be upon him): "O my son! I have seen in a dream that I sacrifice you. See what you think" (37.102)?

The man started shaking and farted loudly! Those present, as well as myself, were all stunned. I repeated the question hoping to help him cover up what he had just done, but he produced the loud noise again and defecated on himself. Drops started to show on his thighs and the place became full of a repulsive smell. He prostrated and said: "Forgive me for Allah's sake. I have overstepped my limits. I will go to Shaikh ʿAbd al-Qādir al-Gaylānī to ask for Allah's forgiveness, but if He does not grant me forgiveness, I will kill myself." I said: "Come and take the pledge, repent to Allah, and start with the dhikrs. This is sufficient." He went and took off his dirty clothes, remaining only in a long shirt, performed ablution, and came back and took the pledge.

Family Who Came to Test the Caliph

Date: 2014

Location: Kanaka Nagar - Bangalore - Karnataka

When one day I came back from a preaching journey, I found three young families waiting for me. I greeted them and entered the house. They followed me to salute me by kissing my hand, but I apologized as I was exhausted. At times I leave at dawn, and, at times I walk for two or three days in each preaching journey. I sat on my chair while they sat in a semi-circle.

I had bowed my head, in contemplation of my Shaikh, when I felt the presence of a table fan on my left. It was rotating, pushing air towards me every time it came into my direction. I thought about how there was no fan in this house, and I started wondering who could have put it in here so quickly. I opened my eyes and raised my head slowly towards the left, but I did not see a fan. However, the voice of the Shaikh filled my head with the following words:

> On your right there is a man who has come to test you. Do not be afraid, for I am with you. The woman next to him is his mother. She is suffering from an illness in her legs. Her treatment is as follows (he described it). The lady next to the old woman is the man's wife. She has a pain in her right ear. Her treatment is as follows (he described it). Now start talking to them.

Both women were veiled. I turned towards the man and saluted him; he returned the greeting. I asked him his name; he replied "Wazīr." I asked him about his job, and he said that he was a wood merchant. I said to him: "Glory be to Allah. Is the woman next to you your mother?" He said: "Yes." I said: "Is the woman next to her your wife?" He said: "Yes." I said: "Does your mother suffer from a pain from her knees to her feet? She should use the following treatment (I prescribed what the Shaikh told me). You wife has a problem in her right ear. She should use the following treatment (I prescribed what the Shaikh told me)." At this point, the man started sobbing and threw himself at my feet. I went on to say: "In addition, you have come to test me." He said: "I swear by Allah the great that you are a Shaikh….etc. Everything is exactly as you said. My intention was to test you in front of my mother and wife." Wazir became my right-hand man in Bangalore.

Opponent of Celebrating the Birthday of the Prophet

Date: 20/5/2015
Location: Salempur - Delhi

A group of twelve men gathered at my house. The group consisted of three scholars, two muezzins, and seven trustees. They had some questions, and they started with standard sceptical ones. One of them then asked about celebrating the birthday of the Prophet (*ṣallā Allah ʿalaihi wa sallam*), arguing that it is prohibited. Ḥaḍrat Shaikh Muḥammad al-Kasnazān put in my heart something that made me and the others laugh. I asked that person: "Do I know you?" He replied in the negative. I asked him: "How many children do you have?" He replied: "I have one boy whose name is ʿAbd al-ʿAzīz." When I asked him his age, he said that he had completed his first year five days ago. I said: "Congratulations, O brother! Did his mother throw a birthday party for him and sing 'happy birthday to you'?" He replied in the affirmative. I said: "As a scholar, how do you justify permitting the celebration of the birth of an ordinary child while prohibiting people from celebrating the birth of he who saved the world from the evil of delusion and the darkness of ignorance?" He said: "What have I done to myself? Who taught you this?" I replied: "The one who sent me to you, my Master Shaikh Muḥammad al-Kasnazān." After three hours of discussion, eleven of the twelve men took the pledge, and the other man said he had taken the pledge of another Ṭarīqa in the past.

Impure Reader of the Qur'an

Date: 27/5/2015
Location: Jaipur

A mufti to whom I had given the pledge invited me to a school called "Ḥanafiyya Madrasa," which taught the memorization of the Qur'an. He asked me not to speak about the Ṭarīqa because of the mentality of the people at the school. After I met the students, one of them asked me from a paper of questions that he was holding:

> How can you say that the Prophet (*ṣallā Allah ʿalaihi wa sallam*) is a light when Allah says in the Qur'an: "Say: 'I am only a human like you'" (18.110)?

I criticized his understanding of the phrase "like you," telling him:

> I ask for forgiveness from Allah. Can you see behind you like you see in front of you?

This argument is a reference to the fact documented in the biography of the Prophet (*ṣallā Allah ʿalaihi wa sallam*) that he saw behind him as he saw in front of him. I then continued the argument with this sceptic about the light of the Prophet until I exposed him by saying:

> Stand up and swear in front of everyone that you have ablution and that you do not go to sleep while you are in need of purification after having intercourse? Stand up and swear if you can!

The man did not say a single word, having been disgraced by Allah. He folded his paper, put it in his pocket, and lowered his head. I continued the preaching and spoke about the Ṭarīqa until fifty people took the pledge. The mufti also praised the preaching.

4

The Unique Status of the Shaikhs of Ṭarīqa Kasnazāniyya

The karāmas in this chapter show the unique status of the Shaikhs of Ṭarīqa Kasnazāniyya, represented by the present Master Shaikh Muḥammad al-Kasnazān, as the true advocates of the way of the Prophet (*ṣallā Allah ʿalaihi wa sallam*).

Shaikh Muḥammad al-Kasnazān is the Deputy of the Prophet

Date: 10/10/2012
Location: Saraipalya - Bangalore - Karnataka

A car broke down in front of the door to the fenced land of the takya. Three men got out and started looking at the flag of the takya while I was looking at them. I later learned that one of them was a businessman, the second an engineer, and the third a professor of Sufism whose name was Ḥaidar ʿAlī. They came in and asked about the place, so I explained that it was a takya of Ṭarīqa ʿAliyya Qādiriyya Kasnazāniyya, whose Master is Shaikh Muḥammad al-Kasnazān al-Ḥusseinī (May Allah sanctify his secret), who is the Ghawth of the time.

I told the professor that I would like to ask him a question: "Was it your knowledge or ours that brought you to us?" He asked me to repeat the question. I asked again: "Was it your knowledge or ours, which we take from the All-Knowing, which brought you to us?" The professor did not understand the question. I asked him to sit next to me. His left hand was in a splint due to a fracture. I told him that I would like to give them the pledge, so he asked about it. I started talking about the necessity of having a pledge with a perfect Shaikh, and I started describing what a perfect Shaikh was like. My words touched him so he said that he wanted to take the pledge. I told them that their car will be ready to start after they took the pledge. He said: "Let's see if what you say is true," and they took the pledge.

The professor asked whether the car would start now. I replied in the affirmative, saying that Allah had achieved the good that He wanted for them. They wanted to open the bonnet of the car to examine it, but I told them not to do so as I promised that it would start. I asked them to get into the car, close the doors, and start the engine. The professor said: "Let's check it first," but I insisted: "No need to check. If the car will not start, then I am a liar." They did as I asked them to do, and the car did indeed start. Impressed by what happened, the professor disembarked, kissed my hand and foot, and donated five thousand rupees to the takya. He said in astonishment: "How did this happen?" I said: "This is Ṭarīqa Kasnazāniyya." He said that he would keep in touch as his house was nearby.

The professor came again next day with four or five people. He knelt at the door of the takya before entering.

He introduced his companions as friends, before going on to say that he wanted to talk about what happened to him the day before. I thought the professor wanted to recount to his friends the incident of starting the car, but I was completely surprised by what he had to say:

> O caliph! After I left yesterday, some doubts developed in my heart. I am a professor of Sufism, so how can this person teach me, give me the pledge… etc.? I felt envious. When I arrived home, I was tired, so I slept. I had a dream in which I saw this same place of the takya and you were sitting in this place and position. As I started getting closer to you, I was surprised that the face was not yours, but that of an older person. That person then called to me, so I sat next to him. He started to say to me the same things you told me. I thought and said to him: "Sir, I heard these words yesterday from someone who was sitting here. He was wearing similar clothes and green cloth, but his face was different." The person replied: "Yes, that is the caliph of Shaikh Muḥammad al-Kasnazān. I am ʿAlī bin Abī Ṭālib, the caliph of the Messenger of Allah. Because you put your hand in the hand of the deputy of Shaikh Muḥammad you have put your hand in ours."

The professor started to cry, some of his companions fell into a state of submissiveness, and one of them cried. The professor said that Imam ʿAlī bin Abī Ṭālib went on to say:

> We are the family of the house of prophethood. No one on this earth or in the universe has the right to speak on our behalf other than our heir Shaikh Muḥammad ʿAbd al-Karīm al-Kasnazān.

I was stunned to hear this. The professor then said that he would like the friends who came with him to take the pledge and gain the good that he had tasted.

On the same day, I phoned the Shaikh's servant to tell him about this karāma. He told me that ḥaḍrat Shaikh Muḥammad had said on the previous night that no one but Shaikh Muḥammad al-Kasnazān has the right to speak on behalf of the house of the Prophet (*ṣallā Allah ʿalaihi wa sallam*).

Gift from the Prophet to Shaikh Muḥammad al-Kasnazān

Date: Beginning of 2013
Location: Shadab Nagar - Bangalore - Karnataka

I was waiting before the dawn prayer for a phone call from Medina when I dozed off. I saw in my dream a man from Medina present to me an extremely beautiful frame made of gold. It contained a board made of thin wood and covered by a green cloth. The following text was written on two lines and on part of a third line on the cloth:

> From Muḥammad the Messenger of Allah to my son, my beloved, and my spirit, Muḥammad ʿAbd al-Karīm ʿAbd al-Qādir.

There were other writings, maybe names, underneath, but they were not clear to me. The frame was rather heavy, but I carried it and was very happy with it. I kissed it several times and wanted to bring it to the Shaikh.

I was then woken up by the phone call from Medina I was waiting for. I heard over the phone the call to the dawn prayer there. The time in India was quarter past eight in the morning.

Shaikh Muḥammad al-Kasnazān is the Promoter of the Tradition of the Prophet

Date: 11/9/2013

Location: Shadab Nagar - Bangalore - Karnataka

I was waiting for the time of the afternoon prayer when I was overcome by sleep. I had a dream in which I saw myself in Medina. I was standing at the end of a long queue of people. We were all waiting for the Prophet (*ṣallā Allah ʿalaihi wa sallam*) to come out from his shrine under the green dome so that we could visit him. Suddenly, everybody turned toward me and said: "Come close, for the Prophet (*ṣallā Allah ʿalaihi wa sallam*) has asked for you." I also turned my head to see if these people were addressing someone behind me, but there was no one. The waiting column then split into two on both sides to allow me to come forward. I walked shyly. I saw the Prophet (*ṣallā Allah ʿalaihi wa sallam*) standing near to the door. He looked tired and was leaning on ḥaḍrat Shaikh Muḥammad al-Kasnazān for support. The Shaikh had his right hand behind the Prophet's back and under his right armpit. The Prophet (*ṣallā Allah ʿalaihi wa sallam*) had his left hand on ḥaḍrat Shaikh Muḥammad's shoulder. I said: "Allah is greater! The Prophet (*ṣallā Allah ʿalaihi wa sallam*) is tired? Why?" The Shaikh indicated to me with his noble head to come closer. Before I got closer, I could see some of the Prophet's (*ṣallā Allah ʿalaihi wa sallam*) face, but as I moved closer, thick clouds gathered on him and the Shaikh, and I could not see any parts of them other than the Shaikh's face. When I was closer, I heard the Prophet (*ṣallā Allah ʿalaihi wa sallam*) say: "Only he lifted me," meaning Shaikh Muḥammad. I understood this to mean that the Shaikh is the promoter of the way of the Prophet (*ṣallā Allah ʿalaihi wa sallam*) — something I was already certain of.

5

Mysterious Visitors

Each of these karāmas features an encounter between the caliph and a mystical character.

Khidhr[20]

Date: 2011

Location: Bangalore - Karnataka

In the first year of preaching in India, I was invited to a celebration of the birth of ḥaḍrat Shaikh ʿAbd al-Qādir al-Gaylānī in the house of a late caliph. Those who invited me loved the Ṭarīqa but they had not taken the pledge, and they did not practice. They did not pay much attention to the Hereafter, restricting their worship to performing the Friday prayer. But I liked the house and felt happy there because it had traces of the Ṭarīqa, even though it had no traces of worship. Tracing the relics of the Shaikhs pleases me greatly. After I finished preaching, many people took the pledge. There were clerics, Imams, and people wearing green clothes,

[20] Khidhr is a very high ranking Walī who has been alive for many centuries. He is believed to be the man whom Allah sent Prophet Moses to meet and learn from, and whom Allah described as: "A servant from among Our servants to whom We have given mercy from Us and whom We had taught a special knowledge from Us" (17/65).

indicating that they had taken the pledge of a Ṭarīqa that goes back to ḥaḍrat Shaikh ʿAbd al-Qādir al-Gaylānī.

After I finished preaching and giving the pledge, people asked me to read ḥaḍrat Shaikh al-Gaylānī's famous poem "al-Khamriyya." It looks like they liked my voice and my speaking style. There were three or four clerics present who spoke Arabic fluently.

While I was reading the poem, a brown man approached me. The lower half of his face from the middle of his nose to his chin looked very much like one of the dervishes of the Ṭarīqa. He had a thin beard, as if it had been carefully drawn. His moustache was carefully trimmed, as if it had been drawn in white. His teeth were white, and he looked over fifty years old. He was very handsome. He wore a jubbah and a turban whose green and black colours overlapped in a pyramid-like shape.

The man approached me and stretched out his hand before reaching me, indicating he wanted to shake hands with me. Many people come to visit me in India. I cannot stand up for everyone who comes to greet me, so I usually greet them while sitting. When people try to come to greet me while I am preaching, I signal to them to sit down and not interrupt me. At times, I ask someone to do this on my behalf. But when this man came close to greet me, I felt as if he obliged me to stand up for him. I stopped reading the poem and stood up. As soon as I shook hands with him, my hand became as small as the large bead of the beads, so his hand extended to my elbow. In other words, his hand became long enough to reach my elbow. I felt an unusual kind of fear, and I felt as if my body became a block of ice. My backbone felt like it had stiffened because of surprise or fear. This was the first time that I had experienced anything like this. My feet started to go numb. The man smiled and embraced me, putting both of his hands behind my back. He pulled me toward him twice, as if trying to fix my back. His breath smelt of amber. He then withdrew his hands and left.

While still standing, I turned to the caliph sitting next to me and asked him about the man. The bewildered caliph replied: "What man?" I told him that I was asking about the man that had just greeted me. I looked at the other people and realized that they had not noticed what had happened, as if it had happened to me in a dream. I asked again about why they thought I stood up, and the answer was that I suddenly stopped reading the poem and stood up. Concerned that they would ridicule me if I persisted with asking, I claimed that my eyes were dazzled and I sat down. But I could not speak after that, so I asked to leave, claiming to be tired. The preaching had finished and people had taken the pledge, so there was no harm in me leaving.

When I left, I was scared because of the feeling of awe that the man left on me as he approached me. I thought he was ḥaḍrat Shaikh ʿAbd al-Qādir al-Gaylānī. When I was being driven back, I tried several times to contact the Shaikh's servant. When I arrived at my house, then in Sudama Nagar, the servant called me and asked what was behind my repeated calls. I told him I was scared. I then heard the Shaikh ask the servant about the caller. When the servant told him, the Shaikh asked him to listen to what I had to say. I then started telling the servant what happened while he conveyed it to the Shaikh. The Shaikh said:

> This is Allah's will. Tell him not to be afraid. His visitor was our master Khidhr. Congratulations, congratulations! Let's continue talking tomorrow.

The following night, the servant called to let me know that the Shaikh said the following:

> Many caliphs, dervishes, and Walīs wanted to see our master Khidhr but they did not. It is the spiritual power of the Shaikhs that enabled ʿImād to see him. Congratulations to him. Let him be cautious about himself.

The Shaikh has advised me not to pay much attention to such spiritual experiences, because they are not the foundations of the Ṭarīqa. Its foundations are piety, performing the dhikrs, and adhering to the commandments and prohibitions of Sharīʿa and the Ṭarīqa.

Messenger from the Prophet

Date: 2/11/2012

Location: Kausar Nagar - Bangalore - Karnataka

My living place consisted of a bedroom, sitting room, and bathroom, built on the roof of a house. The roof overlooked the lower floor and a side road, and there were two main roads to the right and left. At 10:50am, I heard a very beautiful voice calling in the Iraqi dialect: "Desire for sale! Lust for sale! Soul for sale! Vagaries for sale!" I thought an Indian who had learned Arabic by working in the Gulf was trying to pull my leg. I rushed to see the person who spoke to me in Arabic in India but I could not find anyone on the roof. I looked down at the side road but it was completely empty; there were no salespeople or any people around at all, although it is usually overcrowded at this time of the day. I thought some roadworks might have prevented the merchants' vehicles from coming through, which is why there were no buyers either. But when I checked, I couldn't see any roadworks. Furthermore, I noticed that the two main roads were as busy as they usually are at that time of the day. Yet the side road looked like it had not been used for twenty years, as if what was happening was dominating the place.

As I was about to walk back to my room, I heard the same voice call: "here, here." It was coming from a tall tree that oversees the house. When I raised my head, I saw in the tree, about one and a half to two metres away, an extremely beautiful bird the size of a partridge. Its colour was a stunning green, but it was not a familiar green colour. Its wings were blue, the top of its head phosphorous dark green, and its beak and legs orange. In visions, at times, one sees a colour that looks familiar but is nevertheless different. I was stunned, and wondered if the voice could have come from the bird. The bird was silent and in a state of terrifying stillness. It bowed its head slowly until its beak was in my direction, then it shook its head left and right making a negatory sign and said: "We will not leave you alone." The bird then flew in the direction of the qibla. My legs could not carry me any longer, and I collapsed and lost consciousness. After waking up, I prostrated in thankfulness to God.

In the night, the Shaikh contacted me through his servant and asked if I had had anything happen to me that day. I said that something very strange had occurred. When he asked about it, I started telling the servant, who was in turn passing on my words to the Shaikh. When the servant told the Shaikh that I saw a bird, the Shaikh interrupted him saying: "This is a messenger from the Prophet (*ṣallā Allah ʿalaihi wa sallam*) to him to strengthen his heart."

Servant of the Ṭarīqa

Date: 7/12/2012

Location: Villages near Kaveripattinam - Krishnagiri - Tamil Nadu

This village is inhabited by mainly Hindus and Muslims and has a mosque. I started preaching to a mixture of Muslims and Hindus and gave the pledge to twenty-one people. I then went to a neighbouring village that does not have a mosque, so its Muslims would come to the first village for the five daily prayers. I gave the pledge to seventeen people.

Before I left the village, four Salafi men came to me. They were accompanied by a fifth man who dressed like them in white clothes and a head cap, but he was distinguishable by his shiny face. I stood up out of respect for the muṣḥaf[21] that was carried by one of them, so all those who were with them followed suit. Standing in veneration of the muṣḥaf is one of the things I learned from my Master Shaikh Muḥammad al-Kasnazān. The person carrying the muṣḥaf said: "Where in the Book of Allah do you find the teaching you have brought?" I said: "What did I bring?" He said: "The Ṭarīqa and dhikrs." I said:

> O brother! Open the Book on the Chapter of Jinn and you will find the Ṭarīqa mentioned in Allah's words: "And if they had remained straight on the Ṭarīqa (Way) We would have provided them to drink in abundance" (72.16).

I asked him: "What is the Ṭarīqa?" He replied: "I don't know." I said: "It is what the honourable Prophet (*ṣallā Allah ʿalaihi wa sallam*) taught about worshipping duties, prohibitions, and commandments." He was taken aback by my reply and became very angry with me. Suddenly, I noticed the man with the shiny face bite his lip and gesture to me, as if asking me to stay calm and not reciprocate with anger. I offered to give them the pledge, but they said: "The shaikh of the mosque has told us not to do that." I argued: "There are many verses on dhikr in the Qur'an, so read them and learn how to get close to Him by remembering Him." They then left.

The strange thing is that they were only four when they left, as by the time the debate ended the good-

---

[21] The "muṣḥaf" is the written Qur'an.

looking man was no longer there. I asked the brothers who were with me about the number of men who came, and they said they were four. I realized that I was the only one who saw the fifth man. When I informed the Shaikh he commented: "This is a commissioned courier of the Ṭarīqa."

Messenger Rain Would Not Touch

Date: 5/11/2012

Location: On the main road between Tamil Nadu and Karnataka

On my way back from a village in which I gave the pledge to twenty-two people, our car broke down. It was raining heavily so I had to stay in the car. I knew that this was a sign from the Shaikhs, so I remained in the car with the driver for two hours. A Muslim fakir[22] knocked on the car window. He looked in his late fifties and had a thin sparse beard, but did not have a distinguished appearance. The fakir greeted me in Arabic: "Peace be upon you." I pulled down the window and returned his greetings. He stretched out his hand, so I gave him five hundred rupees. He surprised me by asking: "How much do you want in return?" I replied: "You decide." He said: "God willing, it will be completed today." I said: "What is it?" He said: "It will be completed," then he walked away. It was then that I noticed that his clothes were completely dry despite the heavy rain, so I got out the

[22] In India, a "fakir" is either a wandering dervish who lives on alms or an itinerant Hindu ascetic.

car and ran after him. I caught him and said: "By God, what is it that will be completed today?" He replied: "The problem about which you came." He then made the sign of a rectangle. I said: "By God, who are you?" He said: "He knows me." I asked: "Who knows you?" He replied: "He" and left. My body was completely soaked with rain, yet not a single drop had fallen on him.

I later asked the Shaikh about the identity of this dervish. He said that they, meaning the Shaikhs, know him and that I shouldn't worry about his identity.

When I was back in the takya, the owners of the land of the takya came to me and said that I must register the land now, otherwise I would lose it. They said that its owner was set to increase its price the following day, as this is the law in India. I went with the caliphs and had the land registered on that day. I should note that the land of the takya is rectangle-shaped, like the sign the fakir made.

6

Expelling Evil Spirits

One of the well-known forms of the blessing of the Ṭarīqa is that the spiritual link with its Shaikhs, through the pledge, keeps bad spiritual creatures, i.e. devils and evil jinns, away from the dervish.

Possessed People

Date: 23/10/2012

Location: Kaveripattinam – Krishnagiri - Tamil Nadu

An affliction inexplicably broke out in the village. The person with this condition produces voices like the hissing of snakes, their skin becomes a pale yellowish colour, they lose their mind, and they lose control of urination and defecation. One person from that village whom I had given the pledge to five months earlier came to see me. He said: "My brother and I have not got this condition, but the other ten members of my twelve-person family and all of our neighbours have it." I asked him how long they have been suffering from this condition, to which he replied: "About a month." I asked him if they had seen the doctors, which he confirmed. He said that they have a children's doctor in the village but that the doctor had also fallen victim to this condition. He claimed that this condition was not a medical illness but some kind of madness caused by evil spirits. When I asked him who told him that, he mentioned a fortune-teller.

I asked him to prepare a place and a quantity of water before I visited him. After he got in touch with me the following morning I made my way to the village. I asked him to bring the patients to me one at a time. I gave each of them the pledge and washed their head with the water after I read a special dhikr over it, which the Shaikh had taught me, which invokes the madad of the chain of the Shaikhs of the Ṭarīqa. After washing the person's head with the water, they became stable. I gave the pledge to forty-two people. The following day some of them visited me at home, having fully recovered, and thanked the Shaikh.

Two Possessed Men

Date: 8/11/2012
Location: Bangarapet - Karnataka

This village is inhabited by both Muslims and Hindus. According to common belief, people in this village get possessed by evil spirits that make the person lose their mind. When I asked them about the symptoms of this condition, they said that it makes the person, whether male or female, take their clothes off because of the pain. They also scratch their body until it starts bleeding. The patient's state is truly miserable. I saw two men with this condition and I gave them the pledge. The first was healed immediately. He regained awareness of himself, time, and place. He started asking why he was there, who I am, and so on. The situation was very touching for his family who started to cry. The second patient improved after about an hour. When he woke up, he started hallucinating.

Possessed Woman

Date: 2014

Location: Kanaka Nagar - Bangalore - Karnataka

Two Hindu families came to see me bringing with them a woman who had a condition of possession similar to those that I had seen before. When I saw her I became afraid, so I started asking for madad from the Shaikh. I invited both families to embrace Islam. They said: "If this woman recovers, we will embrace Islam." The patient started crying and tearing off her clothes, so people came to help and cover her. I looked at the photo of the Shaikh and said: "They have come to your door, and I am your door. I cannot do anything without you."

I said to them: "Bring her back to me." While standing over her, I asked for madad from the Shaikh and recited a dhikr that the Shaikh had granted me permission to use over a glass of water. After drinking the water, the patient calmed down. I gave her the pledge, and she became amazingly quiet. She then said twice: "I bear witness there is no god save Allah," then she said: "I bear witness that Muḥammad is the

Messenger of Allah." All started hailing and some family members began to cry. They then took the pledge and embraced Islam. The caliphs filmed this karāma from the start.

Devils in a Hindu House

Date: 12/1/2013
Location: Kanaka Nagar - Bangalore - Karnataka

A Hindu family came to see me on 6/1/2013. They were suffering from problems, nightmares, and devils in their house. They asked for proof before they embraced Islam. I said: "I can only promise you that, by the spiritual power of Shaikh Muḥammad al-Kasnazān, from today, you will not see any of these bad occurrences. Will you promise to return to take the pledge if my words prove to be true?" They promised. This family came back today with another two girls and all five embraced Islam.

Jinns in a House

Date: 20/9/2014
Location: Kausar Nagar - Bangalore - Karnataka

A family came to see me complaining about the presence of jinns in their house. I said to them:

> My duty is to tell you to take the pledge and teach you how to perform the dhikrs, and also to pray to Allah to protect you, show mercy to you, and remove any evil that has touched you. This is where my duty

> ends and the duty of my and your master, Shaikh Muḥammad al-Kasnazān, starts.

I then gave them printouts of the dhikrs and chain. Two days later, one of them and his two sisters came to seem me. One of the sisters said:

> I saw in a dream a man who said to me: "Start by reciting the dhikr of 'la ilāha illā Allah, Muḥammadun rasūlu Allah' for one hundred and fifty thousand times." I said: "Who are you for me to take orders from you?" He replied: "I am your Shaikh, Shaikh Muḥammad al-Kasnazān, the Shaikh of the human beings and the jinns."

The physical descriptions of the man that the woman gave also matched those of the Shaikh. I told her: "Congratulations on seeing ḥaḍrat Shaikh Muḥammad in a dream! Would you recognize him if you saw him?" She replied in the affirmative, so I showed her three photos, one of ḥaḍrat Shaikh Ḥussein al-Kasnazān, another of ḥaḍrat Shaikh ʿAbd al-Karīm al-Kasnazān, and a third of ḥaḍrat Shaikh Muḥammad al-Kasnazān. She pointed to the latter and said: "This is the person who came to me in the dream." I said: "That is right, congratulations! Start with the dhikr that the Shaikh ordered you to perform. When you complete it, start with the first of the permanent dhikrs of the Ṭarīqa."

When I informed the Shaikh in the evening he asked about what I told the woman to do. I said that I asked her to start with the dhikr that the Shaikh ordered her to do in the dream. He approved of what I said to her and said: "May Allah bless you."

7

Replacing Enmity to the Ṭarīqa with Love

These karāmas show how Allah replaces the hostility to Islam and the Ṭarīqa with love and keenness to embrace Islam and follow the tradition of the Prophet Muḥammad (*ṣallā Allah ʿalaihi wa sallam*).

Juice Turns a Hindu's Enmity to Islam into a Desire to Embrace It

Date: 22/10/2012

Location: Saraipalya - Bangalore - Karnataka

There were eighteen persons in the takya, including a Hindu man. The latter was angry because his cousin had embraced Islam the previous day. He was agitated when he came to ask about what we do. He said accusingly: "What is it that you did yesterday?" I invited him to sit and presented him with some juice that I had been given earlier. I asked him to drink it while I was asking for madad from the Shaikh. As soon as he tasted the juice, he looked at the container. He kept on drinking and looking with surprise at the container. He then asked: "What kind of juice is this?" I replied: "I do not know its ingredients, but it is made in India. It had just been given to me as a present which I presented to you." He asked whether I had added anything to it, but the container was sealed and it was he who opened it. He went on to say: "Trust me, I have never tasted juice like this before." I said: "Look at the container; isn't it similar to other containers?" He said: "Yes, but this is different from what is in the market." He then said:

> I feel all the anger inside me towards you has gone. I did not believe in what you were teaching, but I feel now as if I have drunk faith. How can I become like my cousin?"

I gave him the pledge and he embraced Islam by the blessings of the Shaikh.

Spiritual Instruction to a Hindu Woman to Embrace Islam

Date: 3/12/2012
Location: Village called Nidusali - Tamil Nadu

This village is mainly Hindu; I did not actually see any Muslims there. I started to talk about the aftermath of death, but some men interrupted and ridiculed me. They argued that after death my corpse would be burned and scattered in the air, so there is no punishment or reward after death. I told them that anyone who would like to have a good life after death must lead a principled life in this world. I reminded them how even the kings and the most powerful people could not escape death.

A woman called Angamma, who was known to the people of the village, was also present. She had converted from Hinduism to Islam after being cured of possession by the blessings of the Ṭarīqa. Angamma is a very active dervish who, among other preaching activities, convinced her three sisters and their husbands to embrace Islam and three Salafi men to take the pledge of the Ṭarīqa. Angamma told the gathered people:

> I paid hundreds of thousands of rupees for treatment but even Bangalore's doctors failed to cure me. This man gave me water after reading Qur'anic verses over it and you all know that I have fully recovered. My husband has also come with me and we are both Muslims now. If this man leaves your house without you availing yourselves of the blessings he has, you will regret it.

Nevertheless, only three women took the pledge.

After giving the pledge, I told all that there is no compulsion in Islam, they are my brothers and sisters in humanity, and I am happy to have met them, and I then left. Suddenly, I heard shouting inside the house. When people rushed to the source of the voice, they found an old Hindu woman, who had objected to my preaching early on, shouting loudly: "Bring the man back to me, bring the man back to me." I went to see her and found her shouting:

> Kadavul, Kadavul, Kadavul. Kadavul ordered me to kiss your foot and join you. Kadavul left our house and said: "Call him and take the pledge. My role has just ended."

The word "Kadavul" in Tamil means "God." I gave her the pledge outside the house. All the villagers gathered and I gave them all the pledge. There were two hundred and eighteen people. I was left with no printouts of the dhikrs and chain. There are photos of the villagers after they took the pledge.

The Pledge Purifies the Heart of a Convert from Hinduism

Date: 30/12/2012
Location: Saraipalya - Bangalore - Karnataka

A Hindu man visited me today. He said: "Five years ago I became a Muslim at the hand of a Muslim man from the mosque. But I have not benefited anything from Islam. I still drink alcohol and worship my old god and the other Hindu gods. What is the point in Islam if it does not change me?" I said: "That is right, but do all Hindus have the same creed?" He replied: "No." I said: "Are all equally committed to God?" He also replied in the negative. I said: "This is the case with all other religions. I will now give you proof in front of people."

I asked several times for madad from the Shaikh and then asked him to give me his hand to give him the pledge. As I do when I give the pledge, I asked him to close his eyes, and I closed mine, and then I started reciting the pledge. He became like an innocent child, like a meek lamb. He started crying as I was reading the pledge. After the completion of the pledge, he said loudly: "Allah, Allah." His wife and friends asked him about what happened. He replied: "This man has washed my heart. I now feel like an angel, not a human being." As a result, another two Hindus embraced Islam.

A Muslim Opponent of the Ṭarīqa Becomes a Dervish

Date: 6/1/2013

Location: Saraipalya - Bangalore - Karnataka

A few days ago, I was visited by a man who had just finished working in Saudi Arabia. He was still under the influence of Wahhabi[23] thought. He came out of curiosity, rather than respect, to see what the takya was about. As I talked to him, Allah put His light in his heart and he said:

> Let me be open with you. I came to buy land in this area, but when I learned that there will be a takya, I lost my desire to buy land. But after visiting you and listening to you, the effect of your words on me has been great. By Allah, my brother, I would like to take the pledge, but I would also like all of my family and relatives to come here and see what I saw.

I replied: "I am merely a messenger of Shaikh Muḥammad al-Kasnazān. All that you have heard and seen is due to his spiritual blessings and help." He then took the pledge. Today he came with twenty-nine people from five families and said: "They are all servants of the

---

[23] Wahhabism is a religious movement that was started by Muḥammad bin ʿAbd al-Wahhāb (1703-1793), who lived in today's Saudi Arabia. It is a very narrow interpretation of Islam and a school of thought that accuses many Muslims of polytheism, as it rejects Islamic concepts and practices that are known from the early days of Islam. Wahhabism focuses on appearance and denies the spiritual dimensions of religion, which is why it rejects Sufism.

takya. They have come to take the pledge." I gave them the pledge.

8

Threatening and Punishing Unjust People

We see in these karāmas unjust people being paranormally threatened and punished for their wrongdoing.

Oppressive Husband

Date: 11/10/2014
Location: Tamil Nadu

At the train station of Tamil Nadu, I met a person from a Hindu family whom I had given the pledge to a year earlier. Allah had healed their daughter of possession by evil spirits. Glory be to Allah, his state was very pleasing. He was very observant and fasted the month of Ramadan. He told me the following:

> My brother in law is a Hindu fakir and did not like me embracing Islam. He did not respect his dervish wife either, trying every now and then to create problems. The last of these is that he tried to force her to eat pig meat. She told him: "My teacher, who is the deputy of the Shaikh in India, has taught me to ask for madad from Shaikh Muḥammad al-Kasnazān when I am annoyed by something." Her husband ridiculed her and tried to force her to eat pig meat. She shouted loudly: "O Shaikh Muḥammad, O Shaikh Muḥammad!" and ran towards the door to escape from

the house. When she opened the door she found a giant man who made her stand behind him for protection. He then slapped her husband on his cheek, knocking him down unconscious. He was taken to hospital where he has been unconscious for five days now.

No one, including the wife, knows the man that suddenly appeared at the door. When I asked the Shaikh, he wept and said: "By Allah it was not me but him." I asked the servant who was conveying to me the words of the Shaikh about whom he meant by "him." He said: "I do not know, but he pointed to a mat that has an image of the Shrine of the Prophet (*ṣallā Allah ʿalaihi wa sallam*)."

Man who Betrayed a Trust

Date: 23/9/2013

Location: Kausar Nagar - Bangalore - Karnataka

I was going to take the train to Belgaum in the state of Karnataka, accompanied by a caliph called Jalāl who is very active in serving the Ṭarīqa and preaching. I had given him the preaching license a year earlier. Jalāl had sold a house and received the amount in full, but before we travelled he complained to me. He had asked a blind man to live in that house as a guard, but the man was now refusing to leave the house unless Jalāl gave him the equivalent of five thousand US dollars. Jalāl was sad and did not know what to do. I advised him to go to the authorities, but he said that he could not, because the tenancy agreement between them was not genuine, which is common practice in India. If the man took that agreement to the authorities, they would fine Jalāl the same amount that the man was demanding.

I felt sad for Jalāl and asked him to leave me alone with my Shaikh. Both caliph ʿAbd al-Bashīr and his son Muḥammad Dhākir stayed with me. I stood in front of the photo of the Shaikh and said:

> Beloved! I love this man because he works hard for the Ṭarīqa! I am travelling for preaching and I want the blind man to leave the house before I return from my journey. Beloved! Please do not embarrass me with people!

I kissed the ground under the photo and then read the chapter of Fātiḥa as a present to the Shaikhs of the Ṭarīqa. About two hours later when we were on the train, the blind man phoned Jalāl's wife, who accompanied us for preaching. After she told her husband about the call, Jalāl came to me crying with happiness because the blind man had decided to leave the house after seeing a dream that scared him.

When we returned from the preaching journey four days later, I asked my companions to invite the blind man. When I met him he told me that he had taken the pledge but was not a practicing dervish. He did not even do the daily prayers. I asked him to tell me about his decision to give the house back. This is what he had to say:

> I felt tired and had a headache after the night prayer so I decided to go to bed, although I do not usually sleep this early. As soon as I slept, I heard walking feet. The sound was like iron walking on iron, and it scared me. A man then appeared and said: "Return the

> house to Jalāl, otherwise I will take your soul right now. Do you know who I am?" I could not utter a word, so I asked him silently about his identity. He said: "I am Shaikh Muḥammad al-Kasnazān." He then hit me so hard on my chest that I could hardly breathe. Had I not opened my eyes, I would have died.

I asked him to give me the tenancy agreement and take his stuff out of the house. I gave him a present of eleven thousand rupees.

Man who Desecrated a Photo of Shaikh Muḥammad

Date: 10/2014
Location: Shadab Nagar - Bangalore - Karnataka

Once, as usual, I gave a picture of the Shaikh with printouts of the dhikrs and chain to new dervishes. A few days later, on 18/10/2014, one of those I gave the pledge to came to see me. He looked pale, so I asked him what was wrong with him. He said:

> I ask Allah for forgiveness, I ask Allah for forgiveness. My son tore the photo of the Shaikh and did an abominable thing to it. He afterward suffered internal bleeding and is now in hospital. Also, without prior warning, his wife had today filed for divorce. The court police went to notify him while he was in extensive care. They told him that he should go to the court as soon as he leaves hospital.

I asked why his son did that, and the father replied: "He is a Salafi and hates all photos as they are prohibited according to his doctrine." I told the dervish father: "Your son will not recover unless he comes to me to ask for forgiveness for him, and the Shaikh asks for forgiveness for him, and he takes the pledge." The father said: "I will let him know."

On 21/10/2014, the man came again and said: "My son has died. What do I do now?" I quoted the verse: "We belong to Allah, and to Him we return" (2.256). After the funeral, he brought all of his family and they took the pledge.

Of course, I did not tell the Shaikh what the son exactly did to the photo. I only said that he had transgressed against it. The Shaikh asked me why I did not forgive him. I replied: "Had he come to me or even made a gesture of asking for forgiveness, I would have forgiven him. He rather transgressed and did not repent, so I did not forgive him." After some time, the father came and said: "All that I ask for is that the Shaikh prays for him so he does not end up in hell."

9

Dreams Revealing the Locations of Future Takyas

These karāmas show the Shaikhs' choice of the locations of two takyas and how they revealed them to the caliph in dreams.

The Location of the Bangalore Takya

Date: 6/2011

Location: Saraipalya - Bangalore - Karnataka

When the Shaikh decided to send me to India, he told me:

> Caliph, for twenty years we have been trying to build a takya in Bangalore. Your target is preaching and building a takya.

Following the commandment of my Shaikh, during my preaching journeys I was also looking for some land on which to build the takya. Every time I found a potential candidate, I would tell the Shaikh, but he rejected all that I found, usually because they were too far from where the caliphs and dervishes lived.

One day I saw in a dream the Shaikh driving his old red Land Cruiser, a version from 1990, and I was sitting next to him. He told me: "Son, do you see that lamp with the yellow light?" I said: "Yes," he said: "I want you to get a piece of land in this area." I said: "By the spiritual power of the Shaikh, I will." He went on to say:

> My land is here. I have documents that show that the land is registered under my name. Try and find these documents.

I promised the Shaikh to do so and he drove us off. On our way back, we saw a train pass near that place. I then woke up. From that point on, whenever a piece of land was recommended to me, I would ask whether there was a nearby train track, looking for that sign.

After a while, I saw another dream. This time the Shaikh was sitting in the car while I was standing outside. He was speaking to me through the window. He asked me: "Son, have you found the place?" I answered that I was still searching, I then woke up. When I told the Shaikh about the two dreams he said: "Allah willing, the Shaikhs will give you what you saw."

A week or so later, I was one day in Shadab Nagar, which is in the centre of Bangalore and close to all caliphs. A Muslim estate agent came to me with the paperwork for a piece of land in Saraipalya. I told him that it was too small, as I was looking for a piece of land that was at least one thousand square metres because it was for a takya. He had other adjacent lands, so I told him I needed eighteen to twenty of them. The agent said that they would cost a lot. I had no money then, but I relied on Allah.

I asked him about his name, and he said: "Muḥammad Irshād." When I heard the name, I almost cried. I saw in the name the first sign from my Master that this was the land that was destined to be for the takya. The estate agent's first name, "Muḥammad," is the same as the Shaikh's first name, and his second name, "Irshād," which means "preaching," is the activity of the takya. This and the wonders that followed were also witnessed by caliphs Zakariyya Ibrāhīm Shaikh, Fairūz, and Jaʿfar, the driver.

When we arrived at the piece of land to have a look at it, it was afternoon. I was overwhelmed by a feeling that I cannot explain. I felt like entering Paradise, because we went past a train track. I then saw the street lamp. I told my accompanying caliphs that the lamp was yellow. I told them about the two dreams I saw. I said that the combination of the two signs from the dream that we saw in the land and the fact that the name of the estate agent was "Muḥammad Irshād" was conclusive evidence that this was the land of the takya. The area was overwhelmingly Hindu, with two or three houses of Muslim families. They had a small mosque built out of clay. I told my companions that we would collectively perform the dhikr of afternoon while we waited for the darkness, so that they could see the yellow colour of the lamp. The area was full of mosquitos, so the caliphs wanted to make me change my mind and leave, but I insisted that we waited until it was dark.

At sunset, we collectively performed the sunset prayer. We waited for the street lamps to be lit to see the colour of that lamp, but half an hour passed and the lamps were still off. I asked Fairūz and Jaʿfar to go to the Hindu owner of a small store under the lamp and ask him about why the lamps were not lit and what colour that lamp was. The storeowner said that there was a power cut and they were informed that the power would be back at nine in the evening. He also told them that the lamp was white. I swore a solemn oath that it is yellow. They were astonished by my insistence given that the storeowner would surely know better the colour of the lamp that lit his store!

I told the caliphs that we would stay until the power was back to verify the colour of the lamp. This meant staying at the mercy of the mosquitos for another ninety minutes. After the call to the night prayer, we performed the prayer and the dhikr after the prayer. After a while the power was back. The lamp was indeed white. Zakariyya noted that, so I swore again that the lamp is yellow. Zakariyya laughed hysterically when he saw my immovable belief despite being contradicted not only by the storeowner but even by the eye. But Zakariyya's laughter quickly turned into astonishment when the white light started to turn yellow. It turned out that it was a halogen lamp. I asked the caliphs to go back to the storeowner and ask him why he said the lamp was white. The man came out of the store to look at the lamp. When he saw it, he also was astounded. He said that would swear that it used to be white and that he was completely confident of that because he had had the store for many years.

The other aspect of this wonder, which is the secret behind the Shaikh's identification of the colour of that lamp as yellow, is that all the other lamps were white. It was the only lamp that was yellow! The caliphs cried after seeing this karāma. I repeated to the caliphs my statement that this land was certainly ours. I asked them to start doing the paperwork.

Two days later, Muḥammad Irshād came with another man whom he introduced as the middleman between us and the landlords. I asked him his name and he said "Aḥmad Irshād"! So the signs continued. After we paid the deposit, we went to an office in which we met someone called ʿAbbās, who was the representative of the landlords. After I greeted him, he started kissing my hand and foot, and he pleasantly surprised me when he said that his mother, who had died over fifteen years ago, was a dervish of ḥaḍrat Shaikh ʿAbd al-Karīm al-Kasnazān. She had taken the pledge from caliph ʿAbd ar-Razzāq Sharīf, one of Shaikh ʿAbd al-Karīm's caliphs. Wishing to serve the Ṭarīqa in some way, ʿAbbās said that he would try to get a discount on the price of the square foot of the land.

ʿAbbās then took us to meet a more senior representative who was in charge of many other pieces of land, including the one we would like to purchase. This Muslim man also said that he would like to be of service to the Ṭarīqa because the land would be a takya of Shaikh ʿAbd al-Qādir al-Gaylānī. He offered to bear the costs of the opening ceremony of the takya. I thanked him and asked him his name, just for him to stun me by saying that his name was "Irshād."

When I told ḥaḍrat Shaikh Muḥammad al-Kasnazān that the name of the first person was "Muḥammad

Irshād," the second "Aḥmad Irshād," and the third "Irshād" he commented:

> And your Shaikh is "Quṭb al-Irshād (the Pole of Preaching)", praise be to Allah, and the Ṭarīqa is all about Irshād (preaching). This takya is yours, Allah willing, by the spiritual power of our Master al-Gaylānī, and the spiritual power of Shah al-Kasnazān.

Indeed, we bought the land and built the takya, as the Shaikh said and the chain of amazing karāmas indicated.

The Location of the Delhi Takya

Date: 21/3/2015 at 5:23am
Location: Delhi

I saw in my dream a slim, awe-inspiring man. He was in dark blue clothes similar to those of ḥaḍrat Shaikh ʿAbd al-Karīm al-Kasnazān. He was carrying a very tall flag mast. He said to me: "ʿImād, come and insert it into this place." I inserted the mast while he was helping me with the digging and insertion. The place was surrounded by very beautiful buildings. He said to me: "Here you will build our house." I said: "Allah willing." He then turned to me and said: "Have you recognized me, son?" I said: "Master, I think you are Ghawth ʿAbd al-Qādir al-Gaylānī." He said: "Yes, I am ʿAbd al-Qādir of the drum."[24] He then stretched out his hand, so I kissed it and kissed his noble foot. I woke up with his scent still filling my nostrils.

---

[24] As mentioned earlier, the drum was introduced to the dhikr by Shaikh ʿAbd al-Qādir al-Gaylānī.

When I informed the Shaikh about this dream on the same day, the Shaikh's servant came back to me with the following message from the Shaikh: "Allah willing, He must not come back before founding a takya in the same place that he saw in the dream."

10

Miscellaneous Dreams

These karāmas include dreams about various matters.

Fulfilment of a Dream about the Questioning of the Day of Judgement

Date: 18/10/2012

Location: Village near Yabinpilli - Tamil Nadu

I saw processions that paraded a huge statue of an elephant with the body of a man and were accompanied by loud music and dance. When I asked about it, I was told that it is the god Ganesha, whom people have various stories about.

Strangely, many people came to greet me, some sat and listened to what I was talking about, and others took the pledge from me. I asked one of them, who was a handsome young man, about what they were doing. He replied: "This is our god. We pray to him and offer him sacrifices." He sounded to me as if he was talking about the Quraish[25] before the mission of the Prophet (*ṣallā Allah ʿalaihi wa sallam*). I said to him: "Would you like

---

[25] The Quraish was the tribe of the Prophet (*ṣallā Allah ʿalaihi wa sallam*). They were worshipping several gods besides Allah when the Qur'an was revealed.

to embrace Islam?" He was surprised and refused. I asked him about the reason, so he said: "All I know is that it is the source of all problems in the world." I was surprised by this impression and asked him: "Have you heard of Shaikh ʿAbd al-Qādir al-Gaylānī?" He said: "Yes, he is a god or semi-god for the fakirs." I said he is only a servant, not a god, but God supported him with karāmas because he was one of the greatest Walīs. He asked: "Would you be able to show me any such karāmas?" I said: "Yes, but what would you do after witnessing it?" He replied: "What would you want?" I said: "I want you to embrace Islam, abandon the gods and idols you worship, and become a good servant. After death you will stand before Allah, naked, barefoot, and powerless. He will ask you about your deeds. If they were good, you will enter Paradise, otherwise you will go to Hell." He was immensely touched by these words and his eyes became tearful, which I understood when he revealed the following:

> I am not lying to you, but yesterday I saw a dream in which I was naked and barefoot in an accused box. A voice I could not tell the source of was questioning me. I now understand. Give me the pledge and I will embrace Islam even before seeing the dhikrs.

He took the pledge.

Dream about Imam ʿAlī bin Abī Ṭālib

Date: 12/10/2013

Location: Kausar Nagar - Bangalore - Karnataka

I saw in a dream as if I was lying down in my private room. A very handsome man came in. I stood up in respect to him. He asked: "How are you 'Imād?" I replied: "I am well, sir, thanks to Allah and the blessing of the Shaikhs." I could not say more. He asked again: "What do you want?" I replied: "Sir, I would like the Shaikh to be happy, the preaching to continue, the Ṭarīqa to become established in India, and Shaikh Nahro[26] to succeed." I started to mention the Shaikh's sons one after another in front of him while he was smiling. Then he said: "Open your hand." When I did this, he pressed his right thumb on my right palm. I squeezed his finger with my hand, then he pulled his hand away smoothly and left. I tried to follow him to ask him about his identity, but I could not find him. When I opened my hand I found the name "'Alī bin Abī Ṭālib" written on my palm. I woke up and I was crying so much.

The Shaikhs' Support for the Caliph

Date: 25/3/2015, Morning
Location: Delhi

This happened when I was on a preaching journey. Today I saw in a dream the Shaikh surrounded by mountains of rubbish. He was sitting, accompanied by a

[26] Shaikh Dr Nahro is the eldest son of Shaikh Muḥammad al-Kasnazān and his general deputy. He has been named by his father as the Master of the Ṭarīqa after him.

few people. My heart was full of sorrow for him, but he did not care about the rubbish that surrounded him. He gestured to me so I came quickly. He said:

> Never mind: "He knows the secret and what is even more hidden" (20.7). I know you are sad because of the small number of people who are taking the pledge. I also know how difficult Delhi is. But continue to work, and I and another thirty-three Shaikhs[27] will keep our eyes on you.

He gave me a very beautiful ring and said: "Put it on," which I did. It felt as if it had been made to fit precisely on my finger. I then woke up.

Phone Messages Instructing the Caliph to Go to an Unknown Place

Date: 28/3/2015

Location: Salempur - Delhi

Ten days ago, I saw in a dream that I had received a text message on my mobile phone. The message arrived from a private number and consisted only of one word: "Come!" Four days later, I saw in a dream a second text message with the following text: "'Imād, come!" Baffled and unsure what to do, I only informed caliph Zakariyya. Who is sending these messages? Where am I supposed to go?

The message was repeated in a voice call yesterday.

---

[27] As mentioned in the introduction about Ṭarīqa Kasnazāniyya, the first line of Shaikhs of the Ṭarīqa, which is that of the family of the Prophet (*ṣallā Allah 'alaihi wa sallam*), has thirty-four Shaikhs after the Prophet.

The voice was like the Shaikh's, but it was not his. The voice said: "'Imād, come to al-Wardiyya!" I started thinking about whether the Shaikh wanted me to return, because the only place called "al-Wardiyya" I knew of was an area in Iraq.

It occurred to me yesterday to go to Jaipur, which is about 260 km from Delhi. I did not tell the Shaikh about this journey. I went to do some preaching, as I felt psychologically drained in Delhi. A caliph called 'Āsaf accompanied me. On our way, 'Āsaf asked me if I knew Bangalore's nickname, to which I replied in the negative. He said: "Green City." He then asked me about the nickname of the city of Jaipur, which I also did not know. He said: "Pink City." Despite his attempts to explain the meaning of the name to me, I could not understand it, as I do not know English. But the meaning became clear to me when we arrived at the city and I saw the colour pink everywhere. At this point, I realized that it was the city that the mobile messages talked about it, as the feminine name "al-Wardiyya" means "the pink one."[28] As a result of this and subsequent visits, there are now thousands of dervishes in Jaipur.

---

[28] In 1876, the Mahraja of Jaipur painted the whole city in pink to welcome the visit of the British crown prince, as pink is the colour of hospitality. The city has maintained its pink colour since.

11

Miscellaneous Karāmas

These karāmas do not belong to any of the categories we covered earlier, so we have compiled them in this chapter.

The Shaikhs' Support for the Preaching Dervish

Date: 2011

Location: Bangalore - Karnataka

When ḥaḍrat Shaikh Muḥammad al-Kasnazān sends someone to preach, he supports them with spiritual powers and blessings. When he sent me to India, he said to me:

> Go, and I and thirty-three Shaikhs, from the Prophet (*ṣallā Allah ʿalaihi wa sallam*), are behind you.

In every preaching trip I feel as strong as a walking mountain. At times I used to be scared of myself, because the blessings used to make me feel like a lion. I never felt afraid of anyone or anything.

In each visit to India, I stay about six months. After the end of my second or third visit, while I was at the airport waiting to fly back and some caliphs and dervishes came to bid me farewell, something strange happened. When I went through the body security scanner, it went off. As usual in such circumstances, the officer asked me to go back and remove any metallic objects I had on me. Indeed, I found a key that I had forgotten in my pocket. When I went through the scanner again, I felt all that paranormal power leave me. It felt as if it was withdrawn from me. I recounted this karāma to the Shaikh in the presence of many scholars who were visiting him and asked him about its interpretation. He said:

> This is the spiritual power of the Shaikhs. They give it to you when you need it and they withdraw it when you need it no more.

The Shaikh refers here to the dervish's need for this spiritual power when performing the duty of preaching. Among the sayings of the Shaikh that confirms this fact is the following:

> When I send someone to preach, I vest on him the rank of Pole.

Light Rises from the Caliph's Head

Date: 12/10/2012
Location: Yabinbilli - Tamil Nadu

People from three villages gathered here and I gave the pledge to forty people, among whom were ten Hindus. I invited them to Islam and said: "Now only say 'O beloved, Messenger of Allah!'" One Hindu woman who looked just over fifty years old suddenly started crying. When I asked her what made her cry, she said: "I saw a light rises from the top of your head and up into the sky, so I could not control myself." I have taken photos of her while crying.

Releasing a Youth from Detention

Date: 7/1/2013
Location: Saraipalya - Bangalore - Karnataka

After returning from a short preaching visit, I found two women waiting for me and crying. One of them looked scared and said: "I ask you by ʿAbd al-Qādir al-Gaylānī! My son has quarrelled with a Hindu man and he is now in the police station. You know that we are Muslims and the police station is run by Hindus. I have no power or money other than knocking on the door of the Greatest Ghawth." I said: "Go to the flag of the takya and say: 'O Shaikh Muḥammad al-Kasnazān. I want my son from you,' and wait."

After two hours a child who is a neighbour of the woman came to tell her: "I have come to bring the good news to you that your son is now back home." She kissed the takya's floor and left.

The Ṭarīqa Improves the Life of a Disabled Person

Date: 16/8/2014
Location: Belgaum - Karnataka

Last year I went to Belgaum where I gave the pledge to a number of people. There was a family that consisted of a grandfather, mother, father, sons, and one daughter who had taken the pledge of Ṭarīqa Junaidiyya. One of the sons was a young man who was disabled from birth. His hands were folded behind his back, his legs were twisted, and he could only move his head, but he was intelligent and spoke fluently. I was surprised when I saw that he was the size of a doll despite being seventeen years old. I thought to myself: "What can I do for this child? O Lord, do not embarrass me; O Shaikh, do not embarrass me, for the sake of the Prophet (*ṣallā Allah ʿalaihi wa sallam*)!"

After they have all taken the pledge, the disabled youth said to me: "Can the Ṭarīqa change my life?" I said: "If you are truthful in your dealings with Allah, then yes, the Ṭarīqa will completely change your life." He asked: "How?" I said:

> This is in the hand of "the One who can do anything He wants" (2.253), not in my hand. I am no more than a courier who carries messages. Having taken the pledge, if you and your family be truthful, Allah will change your life, because He says: "Allah does not change the state of a people until they change themselves" (13.11).

When I returned to Belgaum this year, I was pleasantly surprised to find this youth and all of his family among the people who had gathered to take the pledge from me. After all took the pledge, he asked me if he could speak, so I gave him permission. He said:

> Last year, the caliph came from Baghdad and I asked him to change my life. He said that it is Allah who will change your life if you change the way you deal with him. I and all of my family took the pledge from caliph

ʿImād, and we continued to perform the dhikrs. After four months, during which we were competing over who finished the dhikrs first, the commission for disabled people in Karnataka visited me at home. They said: "We have chosen you to represent Karnataka in Britain." My visit to Britain was funded by the state. They tested my computer skills and my skills to make electric transformers, and I won a contest. I also showed them how I could swim, which both surprised and delighted them. They awarded me a gold medal and five thousand dollars. Furthermore, the Chief Minister of Karnataka gave me a house in my name in Belgaum. This is the power of Ṭarīqa Kasnazāniyya and its dhikrs and Shaikhs. Yes, it has changed my and my family's lives.

Shaikh Muḥammad al-Kasnazān's Voice Admonishes a Son Who Disrespected His Father

Date: 2013

Location: On the way from Bangalore to Kolar - Karnataka

I went to preach with the driver and the late caliph ʿAbd al-Bashīr (may Allah show mercy on him) and his son Muḥammad Dhākir. On my way, I contacted the Shaikh's servant who was then with the Shaikh. I told him that I had gone out to preach and needed help with a problem, which I explained to him. There was a married woman who had been a dervish for some time. She was suffering from a shake in her hands and feet and could not sleep. I heard the Shaikh tell the servant to ask me: "Did this condition start before or after she joined the

Ṭarīqa?" I replied: "It started after she joined the Ṭarīqa." The Shaikh said: "Let her stop doing the permanent dhikrs and do only the daily dhikrs."[29]

While caliph ʿAbd al-Bashīr was informing the family of what the Shaikh had said, an argument ensued between him and his son Muḥammad Dhākir. The latter was arguing that he heard that the dervish should stop the daily dhikrs, whereas the father was rightly saying that she should stop the permanent dhikrs. The argument developed until the son shouted at his father. I immediately heard the Shaikh on my left side say: "Son, 'do good to the parents' (4.36). Tell Dhākir not to anger me." I asked the driver to stop the car and took Dhākir aside and told him: "You have raised your voice to your father. The Shaikh is unhappy with you and says that you must not anger him." Muḥammad Dhākir wept and kissed his father's foot.

---

[29] The "permanent dhikrs" and "daily dhikrs" are two types of dhikrs of Ṭarīqa Kasnazāniyya.

Conclusion

Islamic and historical books are full of karāmas that involve the Companions of the Prophet (*ṣallā Allah ʿalaihi wa sallam*) and Walīs. We have already seen, for instance, the karāma of caliph ʿUmar bin al-Khaṭṭāb when the leader of the Muslim army in Persia heard ʿUmar's call from the mosque's pulpit in Medina. Historical writings also inform us about the many karāmas of Imam ʿAlī bin Abī Ṭālib. One example is that one day before dawn, he said to his son Imam Ḥasan:

> O Son! I saw the Prophet (*ṣallā Allah ʿalaihi wa sallam*) tonight in my dream. I told him: "O Messenger of Allah! How much misconduct and sworn enmity I have received from your nation!" He said: "Pray to Allah to harm them!" I said: "O Lord, replace them for me with better people, and replace me for them with a worse man!"

When Imam ʿAlī's muezzin came to give the call to prayer, the assassin came out and struck Imam ʿAlī on the head with a poisoned sword. Imam ʿAlī died three days later.

One of the Shaikhs with numerous karāmas is the Greatest Ghawth Shaikh ʿAbd al-Qādir al-Gaylānī. A large number of people witnessed his paranormal feats at his school and elsewhere. These karāmas helped the Ṭarīqa spread Islam throughout the world and guide countless people.

Most people today do not believe in karāmas. Many

of those who do, think of them mainly as narratives whose characters are righteous men and women who lived in the past. But the karāmas that this book has compiled show that these paranormal feats will be present as long as Islam is present, and that they will never stop happening. A karāma is one fruit of worshipping Allah and being sincere to Him. The world will never be without Walīs, and Allah's honouring of them with paranormal feats is an unchangeable divine law, hence karāmas will continue to take place.

The karāmas in this book show the blessings that Allah has conferred on the Shaikhs of Ṭarīqa Kasnazāniyya and prove that they follow the way of the Qur'an and the tradition of its Prophet (*ṣallā Allah ʿalaihi wa sallam*). These also confirm that such spiritual experiences are available to anyone who sincerely follows the way to Allah. This is what ḥaḍrat Shaikh ʿAbd al-Qādir al-Gaylānī had to say about the spiritual experiences and paranormal feats that the true seeker of the way of the Prophet (*ṣallā Allah ʿalaihi wa sallam*) tastes:

> The true servant continues to respond to the favours with thankfulness and to the affliction with compliance, admitting his crimes and sins and blaming the lower self, until the footsteps of his heart lead him to his Lord (mighty and glorified is He). He keeps on walking with the steps of good works and repentance from bad deeds until he arrives at the door of his Lord (mighty and glorified is He). He continues to step forward with thankfulness for the favours, and with patience on the afflictions, until he arrives at the door of his Lord (mighty and glorified is He). Once he is there, he will face what no eye has ever seen, no ear

has ever heard, and has never occurred to any human being.[30]

There is no better way to end this enjoyable journey with testimonies to the spiritual power of the Prophet's Ṭarīqa, which the Shaikhs of Ṭarīqa Kasnazāniyya inherited from their great Master and grandfather (*ṣallā Allah ʿalaihi wa sallam*), than the good tidings that Allah has for His Walīs:

> Those who say "Allah is our Lord" and then follow the straight path will have angels descend on them [saying]: "Do not fear and do not grieve, but have the good news of paradise, which you have been promised. We are your allies in this world and the hereafter. You will have in it whatever your souls desire and you will have in it whatever you request — a gift sent down from One who is forgiving, merciful" (Qur'an, 41.30-32)

---

[30] Shaikh ʿAbd Al-Qādir Al-Gaylānī, *Purification of the Mind (Jilā' al-Khāṭir)*, Chapter "The Knowledge of Walīs," pp. 80-81, Birmingham, 2008.

Glossary

These terms and concepts are already explained in the text, but I have compiled them here for easy reference. Arabic words are in italics.

Al-Ghawth al-A'ẓam (the Greatest Ghawth): A title that Allah vested on ḥaḍrat Shaikh 'Abd al-Qādir al-Gaylānī, signifying the fact that he is the greatest of all Ghawths.

Bai'a (Pledge): The process of taking the pledge of the Ṭarīqa. The dervish-to-be puts his hand in the hand of one of the caliphs and recites after them certain statements in which the person declares their repentance to God and pledges to follow the Shaikhs of the Ṭarīqa.

Caliph (*khalīfa*): A follower of the Ṭarīqa to whom the Master has given permission to initiate people on his behalf.

Chikungunya: A viral disease transmitted to humans by infected mosquitoes.

Dengue fever: A mosquito-borne disease caused by the dengue virus. It is found in tropical and sub-tropical regions, including India. Symptoms include fever, headache, muscle and joint pains, and skin rash. In a small proportion of cases the disease develops into the life-threatening "severe dengue" fever.

Dervish: A follower of the Ṭarīqa, i.e. a "Sufi."

Dhikr: A prayer of remembrance of Allah. The term shares the same root with the Arabic words for "remember" and "mention."

Fakir: In India, a fakir is either a wandering dervish who lives on alms or an itinerant Hindu ascetic. The original and broader use of the term, *faqīr*, refers to any dervish. This word, which means "poor man," is derived from the Arabic word "*faqr* (poverty)" in reference to the fakir's renunciation of all things to rely only on Allah.

Fanā' (vanishing): Spiritual development in the Ṭarīqa consists of three consecutive stations of "fanā'" that build on each other. This Sufi concept refers to the disappearance of the distinct self through the extinction of one's will. The three stations are: fanā' in the Shaikh, fanā' in the Prophet (*ṣallā Allah ʿalaihi wa sallam*), and finally fanā' in Allah.

Ghawth: A very high-ranking Walī. The word means "helper," in reference to the fact that a "Ghawth" is someone who has spiritual powers that allow him to paranormally help others.

Jinn: A kind of spiritual being that is made of fire. A jinn may be good or evil.

Karāma: A paranormal feat that is performed or experienced by a Walī.

Kasnazan: A Kurdish term that means "the unseen" or "what no one knows."

Khidhr: A very high-ranking Walī who has been alive for many centuries. He is believed to be the man whom Allah sent Prophet Moses to meet and learn from and whom Allah described as: "A servant from among Our servants to whom We have given mercy from Us and whom We had taught a special knowledge from Us" (17/65).

Madad ("help" or "support"): In Sufism, it refers to the paranormal help and intervention of the Shaikh of the Ṭarīqa using the spiritual powers that Allah gave the Shaikh. This technical use of the term is of Qur'anic origin: "When you [O you who believe!] asked your Lord for help, so He responded to you [saying]: 'I am *mumiddukum* (giving you the *madad*) of one thousand angels in succession'" (8.9).

Mu'jiza: A paranormal feat that is performed or experienced by a Prophet.

Muṣḥaf: The written Qur'an.

Prophet: Someone that Allah draws near to Him and gives revelation to.

Quṭb (Pole): A very high spiritual station in Sufism.

Quṭb al-Irshād (the Pole of Preaching): A very high spiritual position that is occupied by only one Shaikh at any point in time.

Salafi: The term is supposed to refer to a person who follows the example of the early generations of Muslims, but in reality it denotes someone who advocates an unhistorical, narrow interpretation of Islam.

Sayyid: This honorific title indicates that the person is a descendant of the Prophet Muḥammad (*ṣallā Allah 'alaihi wa sallam*).

Shah al-Kasnazān: This Kurdish title means "the Sultan of the unseen." It is the title of ḥaḍrat Shaikh 'Abd al-Karīm Shah al-Kasnazān.

Sharī'a: The legal framework of Islamic law which was revealed in the Qur'an.

Takya: This is the place of worship of the Ṭarīqa. The Kurdish origin of this term is the two words "tak kah" which mean "one" and "place," respectively. "Takya" then means "the place of practicing the oneness of God."

Ṭarīqa: This Arabic word means "way." Technically, it denotes the way to draw near to Allah, which He revealed to the Prophet Muḥammad (*ṣallā Allah ʿalaihi wa sallam*) in the Qur'an and which the Sunna (Tradition) of the Prophet interpreted. The Ṭarīqa as a technical term occurs in the Qur'an in the following verse: "And if they remain straight on the Ṭarīqa (Way), We will provide them water to drink in abundance" (72.16).

Wahhabism: This religious movement advocates a very narrow interpretation of Islam and a school of thought that accuses many Muslims of polytheism, as it rejects Islamic concepts and practices that are known from the early days of Islam.

Walī: Someone who is close to Allah. This nearness makes the person experience and perform karāmas.

Lightning Source UK Ltd.
Milton Keynes UK
UKOW02f1456260815

257568UK00002B/10/P

9 781906 342227